WRITING WITH EASE, REVISED EDITION

Level Three

part of *The Complete Writer*

STUDENT WORKBOOK

By

Susan Wise Bauer
and Susanna Jarrett

WELL-TRAINED MIND PRESS

18021 The Glebe Lane
Charles City, VA 23030
www.welltrainedmind.com

Names: Bauer, Susan Wise, author. | Jarrett, Susanna, author.
Title: Writing with ease. Level three, Student workbook / by Susan Wise Bauer and Susanna Jarrett.
Description: Revised edition. | Charles City, VA : Well-Trained Mind Press, [2025] | Series: Complete writer. | Interest age level: 008-009.
Identifiers: ISBN: 9781944481704 (paperback)
Subjects: LCSH: English language--Rhetoric--Study and teaching (Elementary) | English language--Composition and exercises--Study and teaching (Elementary) | LCGFT: Problems and exercises. | BISAC: EDUCATION / Teaching / Subjects / Language Arts. | JUVENILE NONFICTION / Language Arts / Composition & Creative Writing.
Classification: LCC: LB1576 .B383 2025 | DDC: 372.62/3--dc23

1 2 3 4 5 6 7 8 9 10 Versa 32 31 30 29 28 27 26 25

Cover Design by Shane Klink

CONTENTS

“The Straw, the Coal, and the Bean”

by Jacob and Wilhelm Grimm

This story is a very old fairy tale, written down almost two hundred years ago by two brothers named Jacob and Wilhelm Grimm who wanted to collect ancient stories and keep them alive.

In a village there lived a poor old woman, who had gathered together a dish of beans and wanted to cook them. So she made a fire on her hearth, and so that it might burn the quicker, she added a handful of straw. When she was emptying the beans into the pan, one dropped without her observing it, and lay on the ground beside a straw, and soon afterwards a burning coal from the fire leapt down to the two.

Then the straw said, “Friends, where do you come from, and how did you get here?”

The coal replied, “I sprang out of the fire, and if I had not escaped by sheer force, my death would have been certain. I would have been burnt to ashes.”

The bean said: “I too have escaped with a whole skin, but if the old woman had got me into the pan, I would have been made into soup without any mercy, like all of the others.”

“Nothing good would have happened to me either!” said the straw. “The old woman has destroyed all my brothers in fire and smoke; she seized sixty of them at once, and took their lives. I luckily slipped through her fingers.”

“But what are we to do now?” said the coal.

“I think,” answered the bean, “that since we have so fortunately escaped death, we should keep together like good companions, and go on a journey to a foreign country.”

The coal and the straw agreed, and the three set out on their way together. Soon, however, they came to a little brook, and as there was no bridge, they did not know how they were to get over it.

The straw said: “I will lay myself straight across, and then you can walk over on me as on a bridge.” So the straw stretched itself from one bank to the other, and the coal tripped quite boldly on to the newly-built bridge. But when she had reached the middle, and heard the water rushing beneath her, she was afraid. She stood still, and did not dare go any farther. The straw began to burn, broke in two pieces, and fell into the stream. The coal slipped after her, hissed when she got into the water, and breathed her last.

The bean, who had prudently stayed behind on the shore, could not but laugh at the event. She was unable to stop, and laughed so heartily that she burst.

It would have been all over with the bean, but by good fortune a tailor, who was travelling in search of work, sat down to rest by the brook. As he had a kind heart, he pulled out his needle and thread, and sewed her together.

The bean thanked him most prettily. And, because the tailor used black thread, all beans since then have a black seam.

—Trans. Edgar Taylor and Marian Edwardes, 1823;
some archaic language has been clarified by Susan Wise Bauer

Date ______________________

Name ____

Week 1
Day One

Narration Exercise

From "The Straw, the Coal, and the Bean" by the Brothers Grimm

Date ______________________

Name ____

Week 1
Day Two

Dictation Exercise

"Cat and Mouse in Partnership"

by Jacob and Wilhelm Grimm

A cat became friends with a mouse, and the two decided to keep house together.

"We must store up some food for winter," said the cat. The mouse agreed, and together the two bought a little pot of bacon fat. But they did not know where to put it.

Finally, after much thought, the cat said, "We should store it in the church, for no one dares steal anything from there. We will set it beneath the altar, and not touch it until we are really in need of it."

So the pot was placed in safety. But it was not long before the cat had a great yearning for it, and said to the mouse: "My cousin has brought a little son into the world. He is white with brown spots, and I must go to the christening."

"Yes, yes," answered the mouse, "by all means go."

But the cat had no cousin. She went straight to the church, stole to the pot, and licked the top of the fat off. Then she took a walk upon the roofs of the town and stretched herself in the sun, and not until it was evening did she return home.

"Well, here you are again," said the mouse. "What name did they give the child?"

"Top-off," said the cat quite coolly.

"Top-off!" cried the mouse, "that is a very odd and uncommon name."

"It is no worse than Crumb-stealer," said the cat, "which is the name of your own little nephew."

Before long the cat was seized by another fit of yearning. She said to the mouse: "You must do me a favour, and once more manage the house for a day alone. Another cousin of mine has had a child."

The good mouse consented, but the cat crept behind the town walls to the church, and devoured half the pot of fat.

When she went home the mouse inquired, "And what was the child named?"

"Half-done," answered the cat.

"Half-done!" said the mouse. "I've never heard such a name in my life!"

The cat's mouth soon began to water for some more of the fat. "All good things go in threes," said she. "My third cousin has had a child—a beautiful black kitten with white paws. You will let me go to the christening, won't you?"

This time, the cat entirely emptied the pot of fat. When she returned home at night, the mouse at once asked what name had been given to the third child.

"It will not please you more than the others," said the cat. "He is called All-gone."

"All-gone!" cried the mouse, "that is the strangest name of all!"

After this, no one invited the cat to christenings, but when the winter had come and there was no longer anything to be found outside, the mouse thought of their provision, and said: "Come, cat, we will go and eat our pot of fat—we shall enjoy that."

"Yes," answered the cat, "just as much as sticking our tongues out the window."

They set out on their way. When they arrived, the pot of fat was still in its place, but it was empty.

"Alas!" said the mouse. "Now I see what has happened! You have eaten it all while you were pretending to see your nephews being named! First top-off, then half-done, then—"

"One more word," cried the cat, "and I will eat you too!"

But "All-gone" was already on the mouse's lips. She had barely spoken it when the cat sprang on her, seized her, and swallowed her down. In truth, that is the way of the world!

— Trans. Edgar Taylor and Marian Edwardes, 1823;
some archaic language has been clarified by Susan Wise Bauer

Date ____________________

Name ____________________

Week 1
Day Three

Narration/Dictation Exercise

From "Cat and Mouse in Partnership" by the Brothers Grimm

Date ______________________

Name ____

Week 1
Day Four

Dictation Exercise

Date ______________________

Name ____

Creative Writing

This page is left blank intentionally.

From *Mr. Revere and I*

by Robert Lawson

Mr. Revere and I *is a story about the American revolution—told by Paul Revere's horse, Scheherazade! In the first chapter, we learn that Scheherazade used to be a horse in the British cavalry (mounted soldiers). When British soldiers were sent to the colonies to fight against the American Revolution, Scheherazade and her rider were sent "to occupy the Port of Boston in the Massachusetts Colony" and to help put down the rebellion.*

Scheherazade's rider belonged to a group of soldiers known as the 14th Regiment. All of the horses in the 14th Regiment were put on a ship and sent from England to America. This is Scheherazade's account of her journey.

Ajax is another horse, a "magnificent charger." The "artillery horses" were horses that belonged to another military division which was also being sent to America. A "transport" is a ship designed especially to move men and horses from one place to another; a "ship of the line" is a warship with cannons on both sides. To "pipe-clay" a belt meant to clean it with a very fine, white clay that removed dirt and stains from the leather. "Gaols" is an old-fashioned way to spell "jails." An "Accoutrement" is part of a military uniform that isn't a weapon—like a belt, or a bag for carrying food.

I will not dwell long on the horrors of that trip. It was my first sea voyage, but Ajax, who had made several, said he had seen worse. What *they* could have been like I cannot imagine, for it is hard to conceive of any voyage being worse than ours.

We were quartered in the hold of an extremely old and leaky vessel misnamed the *Glorious*. There was no light and less air. Our hay was moldy, the grain mildewed and weevily, the water unspeakable. Rats were everywhere; they ate the food from under our very noses, they nibbled at our hoofs, they made sleep impossible. Our stalls were never cleaned, and of course currying and brushing were unheard-of.

Our grooms occupied the deck above us and a worse lot could scarce be imagined. They had been plucked from the gaols and prisons to fill out our ranks and fought and caroused unceasingly. Ajax and I were fortunate, for the thug assigned to us had been in prison for horse stealing, so at least he knew *something* of horses, and we fared a bit better than our less lucky companions.

How we envied the artillery horses who were stabled on the open deck of another transport, the *Unfathomable!* Of course they were exposed to the weather, and three were swept overboard in a storm; but I think I envied those three most of all.

From the conversation of the so-called grooms, we learned the make-up of the rest of the expedition. There were four transports for the troops, whose condition was not much better than ours, except that they were given rum three times a day and were allowed to go on deck now and then, weather permitting. They had to be closely watched, however, for many had shown a most unpatriotic tendency to jump overboard. A very fine ship, the *Thunderous*, was given over entirely to the Officers and their servants; and of course we had an escort of four great ships of the line: the *Implacable,* the *Incapable,* the *Impossible* and the *Implausible.*

Our passage consumed only a little more than one month—remarkably fast, Ajax said, but to me it seemed an endless horror. Had I been capable of any feeling at all I should have rejoiced when, on the last day of September, 1768, the everlasting motion stopped and the roaring of the anchor chains shuddered through the ship. As it was, I was too sick and weary to care. I could not be interested when the grooms stumbled below to throw us our horrid evening meal.

We were anchored in Boston Harbor, I gathered. Tomorrow we would land. All troops to be clean-shaven, belts pipe-clayed, arms and accoutrements polished, uniforms pressed, hair powdered....

There was no mention of us horses.

Date ______________________

Name ______________________

Week 2
Day One

Narration Exercise

From *Mr. Revere and I* by Robert Lawson

Date ____________________

Name ____

Week 2
Day Two

Dictation Exercise

From *Mr. Revere and I*

by Robert Lawson

After Scheherazade comes to Boston, the soldier who owns her loses her in a game of dice to the owner of a glue factory, a man named Nat Sime. The white glue you use for projects is made from special chemicals that dry when they are squeezed out into the open air. But in those days, glue was made in factories that boiled up animal hides, bones, and joints. The hides and bones have a sticky protein in them that acts just like your glue does today.

Scheherazade isn't made into glue—but she is forced to pull a cart that collects the hides and bones. In the mornings, she is driven down the fish market to collect fish heads, skins, and bones. This passage describes the rest of her daily routine. Hezekiah is the man who takes care of Scheherazade; Mildred is another horse in the 14th Regiment, and Scheherazade does not like Mildred at all.

There are some unfamiliar words in the story. "Gurry" is an old word for fishheads and bones, all piled together. The "van" of an army division is the group of soldiers right at the front of the division, leading the way. A "wain" is a large farm wagon.

In the afternoon we drove to the slaughterhouse, whence we fetched an equally offensive load of hoofs and horns. Then, apparently, my duties for the day were done. I was fed, rather poorly watered and bedded down for the night. This was to be my daily routine for many months.

While the work was not unduly hard the humiliation was almost too dreadful to bear. In the first place, for a horse of my background and attainments to be put in harness at all was unthinkable. Had I my old strength and spirits, I would have kicked cart and harness to bits before submitting to such an indignity. Then to be hitched to a *cart,* and *such* a cart—its unsavory loads the butt of jeers and insults whenever it appeared on the streets!

Also there was my appearance, which grew steadily more pitiful. Nat Sime was not one to waste money on fancy feed, so mine was both atrocious and scanty. I was always half shod; my coat grew long and matted. Hezekiah, although kindly enough, knew nothing of the care of horses. My stable was seldom cleaned; often he forgot to water me or give me bedding. I developed two collar sores which he did not know how to treat. They became more painful and hideous daily.

Worst of all was the constant dread that someday I would come face to face with my old Regiment. Changed though my appearance was, every horse would surely recognize me, and that would be the last straw; the very thought of it chilled me. I could picture the dismay of Ajax and the sneers of that nasty little

Mildred. I resolved firmly that rather than undergo that ordeal I would first drown myself in the Harbor.

Of course in a town as small as Boston it was inevitable that someday I must encounter my old comrades in arms and one morning the very thing that I had been so dreading came to pass.

We were toiling up Milk Street from the wharfs with our usual load of gurry when I suddenly became aware of the familiar rattle of drums and the squealing of fifes. Raising my drooping head I beheld the proud van of the glorious 14th advancing down the hill in all its majesty. The morning sun winked and glittered on bayonet and buckle, the scarlet coats glowed hotly, the white-gaitered legs rose and fell rhythmically....

For the first time in my life I ran away.

Wheeling sharply I plunged into the first side street, my one thought to regain the docks and hurl myself into the Harbor waters. I did not get very far.

The street was a narrow one and almost blocked by a huge wain toiling up the hill. Cart and wagon locked wheels, then with a great crash the cart, I, Hezekiah and our horrid load piled up in a tangled mass on the sidewalk.

The crash turns out to be a good thing for Scheherazade—she is rescued from the glue factory by the colonial leader Sam Adams, who gives her to Paul Revere so that he can learn how to ride. That's only the beginning of Scheherazade's adventures.

Date ____________________

Name ____________________

Week 2
Day Three

Narration/Dictation Exercise

From *Mr. Revere and I* by Robert Lawson

Date ____________________

Name ____

Week 2
Day Four

Dictation Exercise

Date ____________________

Name ____

Creative Writing

This page is left blank intentionally.

From *And Then What Happened, Paul Revere?*

by Jean Fritz

Last week, you saw what Boston looked like in colonial days—to a horse. Although the story Mr. Revere and I *has many accurate facts in it about the Revolutionary War, the story itself is imaginary. It is "historical fiction"—"historical" because the story takes place during a real time in the past and happens in a real place, "fiction" because the story itself is made up.*

This week, you will read about Paul Revere's Boston from a nonfiction book—one with no made-up stories in it. Nonfiction books that describe the lives of real people are called biographies; this selection comes from the beginning of a biography written by Jean Fritz, called And Then What Happened, Paul Revere?

You will see a series of periods in the middle of the selection, like this:.... These are called "ellipses." Ellipses show you where text has been left out. We shortened this selection so that it would fit more easily into this book by cutting out several paragraphs in the middle.

A "Day Book" was a diary or journal. A "ewer" was a vessel for pouring water, and a "porringer" was a food dish.

In Boston, there was always plenty to see. Ships were constantly coming and going, unloading everything from turtles to chandeliers. Street vendors were constantly crying their wares—everything from fever pills to hair oil to oysters. From time to time there were traveling acrobats, performing monkeys, parades, firework displays, and fistfights.

Once there was a pickled pirate's head on exhibit; once there was a polar bear.

And there was plenty for Paul to do. When he was fifteen years old, his father died, and Paul took over the silversmithing business. He made beads, rings, lockets, bracelets, buttons, medals, pitchers, teapots, spoons, sugar basins, cups, ewers, porringers, shoe buckles, and candlesticks.

Once he made a silver collar for a man's pet squirrel.

To make extra money, he took a job ringing the bells in Christ Church. In Boston, church bells were rung not just on Sundays but three times a day on weekdays, at special hours on holidays and anniversaries, for fires and emergencies, whenever a member of the congregation died, and whenever there was especially good news or especially bad news to announce. Sometimes at a moment's notice word would come that the bells were to be rung, and off Paul would run, his hat clapped to his head, his coattails flying....

Paul had to find new ways to make money. So he engraved portraits, produced bookplates, sold pictures, made picture frames, brought out hymnbooks, and became a dentist. "Artificial Teeth. Paul Revere," he advertised. "He fixes them in such a Manner that they are not only an Ornament, but of real Use in Speaking and Eating."

You would think that with all Paul Revere did, he would make mistakes. But he always remembered to put spouts on his teapots and handles on his cups.

The false teeth that he whittled out of hippopotamus tusk looked just fine.

Generally when he did arithmetic in his Day Book, he got the right answers.

Of course, sometimes there were so many different things to do that he forgot what he was doing. In the beginning of a new Day Book, he wrote, "This is my book for me to—," but he never finished the sentence.

Date ____________________

Name ____________________

Week 3
Day One

Narration Exercise

From *And Then What Happened, Paul Revere?* by Jean Fritz

Date ______________________

Name ____

Week 3
Day Two

Dictation Exercise

From *The Many Rides of Paul Revere*

by James Cross Giblin

This selection is from another biography, The Many Rides of Paul Revere *by James Cross Giblin. Paul Revere and other American colonists were angry because the British government had declared that only one British company, the East India Company, could sell tea in America, and all the money from selling tea would go directly to British merchants. No American merchant could sell tea. A group of colonists who called themselves the Sons of Liberty led the protests against the new British laws.*

Ships filled with cargoes of tea were already sailing toward American ports. The first to arrive in Boston was the *Dartmouth.* The Sons warned its owner not to unload the vessel "on his peril." Twenty-five members of the Sons, armed with muskets and bayonets, stood guard that night to make sure the owner obeyed the warning. Among them was Paul Revere.

The next day, the Sons decided that nearby seaports should be alerted that British tea ships might try to unload at their docks. In a time before the telegraph and telephone had been invented, the only means of speedy communication was a rider on a fast horse. So the Sons assigned five horsemen, including Paul, to carry their urgent message.

Paul must have been an excellent rider for this would be only the first of many rides he would make on behalf of the Revolution. We don't know where he was headed on that December day, or how long it took him to ride there and back. But he must have had to fight weariness all the way, since he'd had no sleep the night before.

In Boston, meanwhile, two more teaships joined the *Dartmouth* at Griffin's Wharf....

That night more than a hundred men, most of them Sons of Liberty, gathered at the wharf where the three tea ships were docked. The men wore ragged clothes and had darkened their faces with soot or lamp black so they would not be recognized. As part of their disguise, many of the men carried tomahawks like those used by Native Americans.

Hundreds of other Bostonians watched from the wharf as the men boarded the first of the ships. After getting the key to the hold, the men hauled the tea chests up onto the deck, broke them open, and hurled them into the water. Once all the tea from the first ship had been disposed of, the men moved on to the other ships and repeated the process. No one tried to stop them. By the time the men had finished, Boston Harbor was awash with tea.

Date ____________________ Name ____________________

Week 3
Day Three

Narration/Dictation Exercise

From *The Many Rides of Paul Revere* by James Cross Giblin

Date

Name

Week 3
Day Four

Dictation Exercise

Date ______________________

Name ______________________

Week 3
Day Five

Creative Writing

From *Homer Price*

by Robert McCloskey

This story happens about seventy years ago. Homer Price lives in the little town of Centerburg. He is going with his friend Freddy and Freddy's little brother Louis to see a movie about their favorite comic-book character, the Super-Duper. They have just heard that the Super-Duper himself is going to be there! Because this story happens a long time ago, Homer and his friends drive to the movie theater in a wagon pulled by their old horse Lucy. In those days, only rich people owned cars!

The Super-Duper's super-stream-lined car was standing in front of the theater. It was long and red, with chromium trimmings, and it had the Super-Duper's monogram on the side. After they had admired the car, they bought three tickets and went inside. There in the lobby was the *real honest-to-goodness* Super-Duper. He shook hands with Freddy and Homer and little brother Louis, and he autographed a card for Freddy, too.

"Mr. Super-Duper, would you please do a little flying through space for us, or mebbe just bend a few horse shoes?" asked Freddy.

"I'm sorry, boys, but I haven't time today," said the Super-Duper with a smile.

So Homer and Freddy and little Louis found three good seats, and ate doughnuts until the picture began.

The picture was called "THE SUPER-DUPER and the ELECTRIC RAY." That was because the villain had a machine that produced an electric ray, and every time he shined it on a skyscraper, or an airplane, the skyscraper or the airplane would explode! He turned the ray on Super-Duper too, but of course the Super-Duper was so tough that it didn't hurt *him.*

Little Louis got so excited, though, that he choked on a doughnut and Homer had to take him to the lobby for a drink of water. But finally the Super-Duper broke the villain's headquarters to bits, and lifted the ray-machine (which must have weighed several tons) and tossed it over a cliff. *Then,* he caught the villain and rescued the pretty girl. But at the very end, the villain stepped away again, and then these words appeared on the screen: "NEXT INSTALLMENT NEXT SATURDAY AFTERNOON!"

"Why did the Super-Duper let the villain get away again?" asked little Louis on the way out.

"I guess that's because he wants to chase him again next Saturday," said Homer.

Outside they admired the Super-Duper's car once more and then started home in the wagon.

It was evening by the time old Lucy, pulling the wagon with Freddy and little Louis and Homer on it, had reached the curve in the road just before you come to Homer's father's filling station.

A car honked from behind and Freddy pulled old Lucy over to the edge of the road. Then, "SWOOSH!" around from the rear sped a long red car with chromium trimmings.

"Gosh! it's the Super-Duper!" said Freddy.

"Well, he shouldn't drive so fast around this curve," said Homer, sort of doubtful like.

Almost before Homer had finished speaking there was a loud screech of brakes, and then a loud crash!

Date ______________________

Name ____

Week 4
Day One

Narration Exercise

From *Homer Price* by Robert McCloskey

Date ______________________

Name ______________________

Week 4
Day Two

Dictation Exercise

From *Homer Price*

by Robert McCloskey

This selection continues the story you read last time.

Then Homer and Freddy and little Louis got out of the wagon and crept along the side of the road.

There, around the curve, was the Super-Duper's car, down in a ditch. All three boys stopped crawling along and lay down on their stomachs to watch.

"Oh, boy," whispered Freddy. "Now we'll get to see the Super-Duper lift it back on the road with one hand!"

There was a flash of light and little Louis cried, "Is that the electric ray?"

"It's only the headlights of a car," said Homer. "Come on, let's go a little closer."

They crept a little closer. They could see the Super-Duper now, sitting there in the twilight with his head in his hands.

"I wonder if he got hurt?" asked Homer.

"Naaw!" whispered Freddy. "Nothing can hurt the Super-Duper because he's too tough."

"Well, if he isn't hurt, why doesn't he lift the car back on the road?" asked Homer.

"Sh-h-h!" said Freddy, "he's an awful modest fellow." So they waited and watched from the bushes.

The Super-Duper sighed a couple of times, and then he got up and started walking around his car.

"Now watch!" said Freddy in a loud whisper. "Oh, boy! Oh, boy!" The Super-Duper didn't lift the car, no, not yet. He looked at the dent that a fence post had made in his shiny red fender, and *then,* the incredible happened. That colossal-osal, gigantic-antic, Super-Duper, that same Super-Duper who defied the elements, who was so strong that he broke up battleships like toothpicks, who was so tough that cannon-balls bounced off his chest, yes, who was *tougher* than steel, he stooped down and said..."Ouch!" Yes, there could be no mistake, he said it again, louder..."OUCH!"

The great Super-Duper had gotten himself caught on a barbed-wire fence!

"Well...well, for crying out loud!" said Freddy.

"What happened?" asked little Louis. "Did he get himself rayed by the villain?"

"Come on, Freddy, let's go and untangle him," said Homer. Then Freddy and little Louis and Homer unsnagged the Super-Duper and he sighed again and said,

"Thank you boys. Do you know if there's a garage near here? It looks as though it will take a wrecking car to get my car out of this ditch."

"Sure, my father has a garage down at the crossing," said Homer.

"And we have a horse right up there on the road. We can pull your car out of the ditch!" said Freddy.

"Well, now, isn't that lucky!" said the Super-Duper with a smile.

So they hitched old Lucy to the car and she pulled and everybody pushed until the car was back on the road.

Date ____________________

Week 4
Day Three

Name ____

Narration/Dictation Exercise

From *Homer Price* by Robert McCloskey

Date ______________________

Name ______________________

Week 4
Day Four

Dictation Exercise

Date ____________________

Name ____

Week 4
Day Five

Creative Writing

This page is left blank intentionally.

Date ____________________

Name ____

Week 5
Day One

Poetry Exercise

"Jabberwocky"
from *Through the Looking Glass*
by Lewis Carroll

This poem is full of made-up words that Lewis Carroll invented just for this poem—like brillig, toves, mimsy, *and* borogoves. *Don't worry about whether or not you're pronouncing the invented words properly, as long as they sound good to you. Don't worry about the blanks and letters to the right of the poem; you will discuss these with your instructor after you read.*

'Twas brillig, and the slithy toves __A__
  Did gyre and gimble in the wabe: __B__
All mimsy were the borogoves, __A__
  And the mome raths outgrabe. __B__

"Beware the Jabberwock, my son! _____
  The jaws that bite, the claws that catch! _____
Beware the Jubjub bird, and shun _____
  The frumious Bandersnatch!" _____

He took his vorpal sword in hand: __A__
  Long time the manxome foe he sought— __B__
So rested he by the Tumtum tree, __C__
  And stood awhile in thought. __B__

And, as in uffish thought he stood, _____
  The Jabberwock, with eyes of flame, _____
Came whiffling through the tulgey wood, _____
  And burbled as it came! _____

One, two! One, two! And through and through _____
  The vorpal blade went snicker-snack! _____
He left it dead, and with its head _____
  He went galumphing back. _____

"And, has thou slain the Jabberwock? _____
  Come to my arms, my beamish boy! _____
O frabjous day! Callooh! Callay!" _____
  He chortled in his joy. _____

'Twas brillig, and the slithy toves _____
  Did gyre and gimble in the wabe; _____
All mimsy were the borogoves, _____
  And the mome raths outgrabe. _____

Quatrain	A set of four lines that belong together
Rhyme scheme	The pattern of rhyming words within each quatrain
Syllable	Part of a word containing one vowel sound
Stress	Where you emphasize a word with your voice
Foot	A certain number of syllables that always fall into the same pattern of stresses

One, **two!** One, **two!** And **through** and **through**
  The **vor**pal **blade** went **snick**er-**snack**!
He **left** it **dead**, and **with** its **head**
  He **went** ga**lumph**ing **back.**

Meter	The rhythm of a poem

Date ____________________

Week 5
Day Two

Name ____

Dictation Exercise

This page is left blank intentionally.

Date ______________________

Name ____

Week 5
Day Three

Poetry Exercise

"Stegosaurus"
by Jack Prelutsky

This poem is from Jack Prelutsky's book Tyrannosaurus Was a Beast. *You will use the blanks at the ends of the lines later in this lesson.*

Stegosaurus was a creature uncontentious and benign, ________
and the row of armored plates upon its back ________
failed to guard its tender belly or protect its flimsy spine— ________
Stegosaurus often wound up as a snack. ________

Stegosaurus blundered calmly through the prehistoric scene, ________
never causing any other creature woe, ________
its brain was somewhat smaller than the average nectarine— ________
Stegosaurus vanished many years ago. ________

1. ______________________

Stego**saur**us **blund**ered **calm**ly **through** the **pre**his**tor**ic **scene,**
never **caus**ing **an**y **o**ther **crea**ture **woe.**

2. unstress **stress** ______________________

3. **stress** unstress trochaic

Date ______________________

Name ______________________

Week 5
Day Four

Dictation Exercise

Date ______________________

Name ______________________________________

Week 5
Day Five

Creative Writing

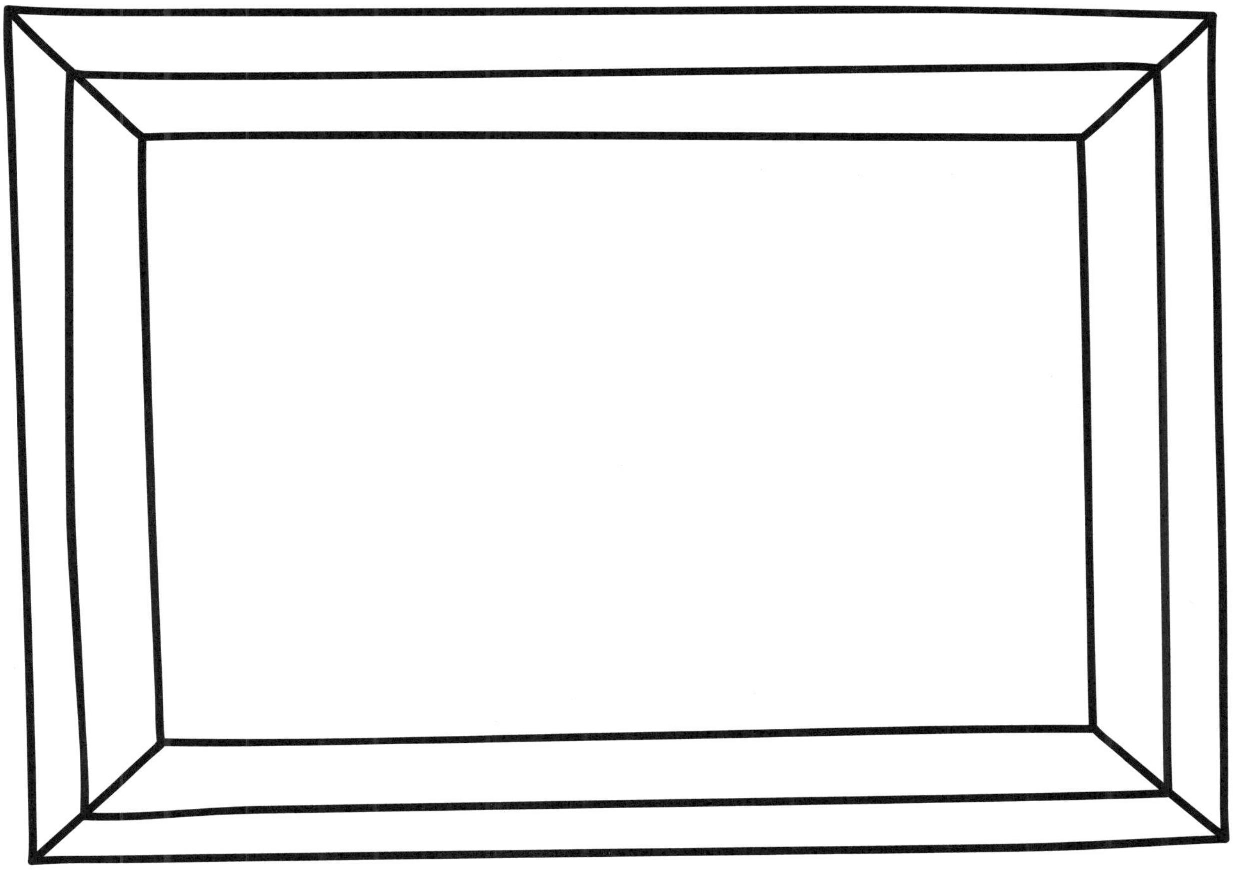

This page is left blank intentionally.

From *Time Cat*

by Lloyd Alexander

In Time Cat, *a boy named Jason discovers that his black cat, Gareth, can travel back in time—and can take Jason with him. The first time the two travel in time together, they end up back in ancient Egypt. They meet the Chief Scribe of the Pharaoh, who offers to take them to the royal residence, the Great House, to meet the king of the Egyptians. But Jason doesn't realize that the Chief Scribe intends to take Gareth for the Pharaoh. In this story, Jason and Gareth have just finished travelling by boat to the Great House.*

At last, the oarsmen docked at the riverbank. The Great House, Jason realized, was a whole city in itself, with bakers, carpenters, brickmakers, weavers. Holding Gareth tightly, Jason followed the Chief Scribe to the biggest building of all. They stopped in one hall filled with nothing but men marking on clay tablets. Here, messengers never ceased hurrying in and shouting commands from King Neter-Khet.

In the space of a few minutes, from what Jason could hear, Neter-Khet had declared five wars, signed three peace treaties, and ordered eight thousand stonemasons to begin a new pyramid. There was also a constant procession of slaves dragging in goods of all kinds. The scribes made a great ceremony of scratching down their tallies. The Egyptians, Jason decided, loved to count things. Nobody, so far as he saw, could do anything without mentioning quantities, writing them down, comparing, adding, and marveling at the totals.

The Chief Scribe approached one of the clerks. "In the records of the Great House make this notation: this day, to the possessions of Pharaoh—life, health, strength—there shall be added forty thousand bushels of grain, seventy thousand jars of oil, three thousand ounces of gold, and one black cat."

"So it was spoken," said the clerk, "so it is written!"

"Oh no it won't!" Jason cried. "My cat isn't one of Pharaoh's possessions!"

"It would seem," said the Chief Scribe, with a cold smile, "that he is now."

Before Jason could turn and race from the hall, the Chief Scribe scooped the bristling, spitting Gareth from his arms. Jason himself was seized from behind, hustled down a corridor, and most unceremoniously shoved into a tiny room.

The heavy stone door swung shut behind him. Jason beat at it with his fists. He had never trusted the oily words of the Chief Scribe. How, Jason thought furiously, had he let himself be tricked so easily? He threw himself against the unyielding door; then, exhausted, dropped to the ground. Now Gareth was gone. Jason would spend the rest of his life in a stone cell in Neter-Khet's palace. The boy hid his face in his hands and his shoulders shook with sobbing. At least, he consoled himself, the Egyptians loved cats and Gareth would be well looked after.

To Jason's surprise, a little while later the door opened and a Sub-minor Scribe peered in. Jason scrambled to his feet. Behind the Sub-minor Scribe were two guards, who took him by the arms and marched him from the cell down one hall of columns after the other, until Jason lost track of them all. In a huge room at the end of one corridor, on a platform topped by a carved and decorated throne, sat King Neter-Khet.

Beside the King stood slaves with fly whisks and feathered fans on jeweled poles, musicians with trumpets and cymbals, and the Chief Scribe himself, looking sour. In front of the throne sat Gareth.

Date ______________________

Name ______________________________________

Week 6
Day One

Narration Exercise

From *Time Cat* by Lloyd Alexander

Date ______________________

Name ____

Week 6
Day Two

Dictation Exercise

From *Time Cat*

by Lloyd Alexander

Jason soon finds out that King Neter-Khet has sent for him because the king has a problem. He likes the cat, Gareth, but he can't get Gareth to do anything he says. He wants Jason to make Gareth obey the royal orders.

"I COMMAND THIS CAT TO PLAY AND ENTERTAIN PHARAOH!" shouted King Neter-Khet at the top of his voice.

The musicians clashed their cymbals. The slaves cried "Life! Health! Strength!" and the fly-whisker whisked as fast as he could.

Gareth did not move.

"Well, go ahead, boy!" hissed the Chief Scribe. "Make the cat be entertaining!"

Jason hesitated, then knelt on the floor beside Gareth. One of the slaves tossed down a toy, a bejeweled mouse on a golden chain. Jason pulled it back and forth in front of the cat, but he could tell from the set of Gareth's ears and whiskers that he was in no mood for games.

Jason dropped the toy and shook his head. "He doesn't want to," he said. "I'm afraid there isn't anything I can do."

Neter-Khet looked angrier than ever.

"I COMMAND THIS CAT TO PURR AND MAKE HIMSELF AGREEABLE TO PHARAOH!" he shouted.

Once again there was a clashing of cymbals and cries of "Life! Health! Strength!"

The Chief Scribe took out a clay tablet. "So it is ordered," he said, "so it is written, and so it shall be done!"

Gareth still did not move. Jason shrugged hopelessly, then picked up Gareth and put him on Neter-Khet's lap. The King began stroking him, but Gareth put down his ears and squinted his eyes. He wriggled out of Pharaoh's arms and leaped to the floor.

"Aiee!" Neter-Khet put his thumb to his mouth. One of Gareth's claws had accidentally scratched the King, and Pharaoh's braided beard shook with rage.

"I'm sorry," Jason said. "He doesn't feel like playing or being agreeable right now. It's nothing personal," he added quickly, "it's the way cats are."

"It's obvious," said the Chief Scribe, "the boy is useless."

"Return the cat to Bubastis," ordered Neter-Khet. "He does not please me. Continue your search."

"And the boy?" asked the Scribe. "The sacred crocodiles are always hungry," he suggested cheerfully.

Neter-Khet closed his eyes and nodded.

"So it is ordered," said the Chief Scribe, making another note on his tablet, "so it shall be done."

Name ______________________ Date ______________________

Narration/Dictation Exercise

From *Time Cat* by Lloyd Alexander

Date ____________________

Name ____________________

Week 6
Day Four

Dictation Exercise

Date ______________________

Week 6
Day Five

Name ____

Creative Writing

This page is left blank intentionally.

From *The Story of the World, Volume 1: Ancient Times*

by Susan Wise Bauer

This excerpt describes one of the great accomplishments of Qin Zheng, a warrior who conquered the battling states of China and made them into one country. These battling states were known as "The Warring States" before Qin Zheng unified them. The word "China" comes from the word "Qin."

When Qin Zheng became the emperor of all China in 221 BC/BCE, he changed his name. From now on, he would be known as "Shi Huangdi." In Chinese, this name means "First Emperor." Qin Zheng, now called Shi Huangdi, wanted his subjects to remember his power every time they spoke his name.

One day Shi Huangdi sat on his throne, thinking about his new empire. He had been careful to stamp out rebellion inside his borders. All of his enemies lived near his palace, and Shi Huangdi had sent his soldiers to guard them and to report on all their activities. He had burned the books that might encourage his people to rebel. He was safe from revolt.

But his kingdom wasn't secure yet. Outside the borders of China, ferocious tribes roved through the wild mountains and plains of the north. For years, these northern barbarians had attacked the Warring States, trying to take over their land. They were the earliest of the tribes which were later called Mongols.

The Mongols rode swift horses and shot arrows with deadly precision. So some of the Warring States had built walls to keep the Mongols out. These walls were still standing, but parts of them had crumbled away into dust. And between the walls were huge gaps.

"The Mongols could come through those gaps at any time," Shi Huangdi thought. "They could sweep down and take over parts of my empire. How can I protect China from the Mongols? If only I could build a wall along the whole northern side of my empire!"

Then Shi Huangdi had an idea: a stupendous, incredible idea. "Perhaps I *can* build a wall along China's northern border," he exclaimed. "A wall thousands of miles long! A *Great* Wall!"

So Shi Huangdi summoned his architects and builders. "All along the northern part of my empire," he told them, "old walls are falling down. I want to repair these walls. And then I want to build a new wall, connecting all the old walls together into one huge barrier that will keep the Mongols out of my kingdom."

"But, Emperor," the architects and builders protested, "there is not enough stone in the far reaches of your kingdom to build a Great Wall!"

"Then think of another way to do it," Shi Huangdi ordered.

The builders and architects labored for weeks trying to think of a way to build the wall in places where stone was scarce. Finally, they discovered a way. The builders made a wooden frame, as high as a man's waist and as wide as a wall. They set this frame upon the ground and filled it with loose dirt. Then workers stamped and packed the earth until it was only four inches high and as hard as concrete. They lifted the frame up, set it on top of the packed dirt, and filled it again. They could build a dirt wall as hard as stone, four inches at a time!

Date ______________________

Name ______________________

Week 7
Day One

Narration Exercise

From *The Story of the World, Volume 1: Ancient Times* by Susan Wise Bauer

Date ______________________

Name ____

Week 7
Day Two

Dictation Exercise

From *The Story of the World, Volume 2: The Middle Ages*
by Susan Wise Bauer

This excerpt, from the second volume of The Story of the World, *describes the Mongols more than a thousand years after the building of the Great Wall.*

The Mongols came from the wild, cold mountains north of China. They lived in felt tents which they took down each morning, leaving nothing but the ashes from their campfires behind. They were nomads who swept over the countryside, conquering and killing. The bone-chilling cold of the north didn't stop them; they wore furs and leather and rubbed their skin with grease to keep the wind away. They never settled down and grew crops; instead they ate foxes, rabbits, and other small wild creatures. But they could go without food for days at a time. If they were in danger of starving, they would open the veins of their horses, drink some blood, and then close the vein and ride on.

The Mongol tribes raided Chinese villages on the northern edge of China. They killed merchants and stole their goods. But they never tried to invade China itself—until Genghis Khan became their leader.

Genghis Khan was born around 1167, into a small Mongol tribe called the Yakka. His father was the Yakka chieftain, or *khan.* But the Yakka was only one of many Mongol clans. And the Mongols fought with each other as often as they fought with the Chinese.

Genghis Khan had a better idea. He thought that the Mongols should all join together and attack China. Just on the other side of the Great Wall lay the rich Chinese city of Beijing, where people lived in warm houses, heated by fires, with soft beds, plenty of food, and bags of gold. Genghis Khan wanted to conquer this rich city.

But first he had to convince all the Mongol tribes to follow him. When his father died, Genghis became leader of the Yakka. He set out at once to conquer the other Mongol clans as well. He fought savagely against them, forcing their leaders to swear allegiance to him. He promised, "Anyone who doesn't follow me will be killed. I will flatten his tent far into the ground, so that a horse galloping across it at midnight won't even stumble. The greatest joy in my life is to kill my rivals and steal their possessions!"

Would *you* surrender to a man who talked like that? Most of the Mongols did. And those who didn't were killed. After Genghis Khan killed one rival leader, he moved his tent to cover the body. Then he ordered his servants to remove the body through the tent's smoke hole, late at night, while everyone was watching the front of the tent. In the morning he announced that the gods had killed his rival and spirited the body away as punishment for defying Genghis Khan. After that, *everyone* followed Genghis.

Now it was time for Genghis Khan to lead the unified Mongols against China. They swarmed down out of the north, destroying every city they came across, leveling every building to the ground. They broke through the Great Wall, into China. And while King John was signing the Magna Carta over in England, Genghis Khan was conquering the city of Beijing.

Date ______________________

Name ____

Week 7
Day Three

Narration/Dictation Exercise

From *The Story of the World, Volume 2: The Middle Ages* by Susan Wise Bauer

Date ______________________

Name ____

Week 7
Day Four

Dictation Exercise

Date ____________________

Name ____

Week 7
Day Five

Creative Writing

This page is left blank intentionally.

From *The Lion, the Witch and the Wardrobe*

by C. S. Lewis

Four children—Peter, Susan, Edmund, and Lucy—have been sent away from London during World War II to stay in the country, which is safer for them. The house where they stay is huge and mysterious. During a game of hide and seek, Lucy (who is the youngest) decides to hide in a wardrobe—a big closet made of wood.

You may not know what a moth-ball is. It is a small hard ball made of chemicals that moths dislike, and moth-balls put in with clothing will keep moths from eating holes in the fabric or fur. In Lucy's day, moth-balls were made from a very smelly chemical called naphthalene.

Looking into the inside, she saw several coats hanging up—mostly long fur coats. There was nothing Lucy liked so much as the smell and feel of fur. She immediately stepped into the wardrobe and got in among the coats and rubbed her face against them, leaving the door open, of course, because she knew that it is very foolish to shut oneself into any wardrobe. Soon she went further in and found that there was a second row of coats hanging up behind the first one. It was almost quite dark in there and she kept her arms stretched out in front of her so as not to bump her face into the back of the wardrobe. She took a step further in—then two or three steps—always expecting to feel woodwork against the tips of her fingers. But she could not feel it.

"This must be a simply enormous wardrobe!" thought Lucy, going still further in and pushing the soft folds of the coats aside to make room for her. Then she noticed that there was something crunching under her feet. "I wonder is that more moth-balls?" she thought, stooping down to feel it with her hands. But instead of feeling the hard, smooth wood of the floor of the wardrobe, she felt something soft and powdery and extremely cold. "This is very queer," she said, and went on a step or two further.

Next moment she found that what was rubbing against her face and hands was no longer soft fur but something hard and rough and even prickly. "Why, it is just like branches of trees!" exclaimed Lucy. And then she saw that there was a light ahead of her; not a few inches away where the back of the wardrobe ought to have been, but a long way off. Something cold and soft was falling on her. A moment later she found that she was standing in the middle of a wood at night-time with snow under her feet and snowflakes falling through the air.

Lucy felt a little frightened, but she felt very inquisitive and excited as well. She looked back over her shoulder and there, between the dark tree-trunks, she could still see the open doorway of the wardrobe and even catch a glimpse of the empty room from which she had set out. (She had, of course, left the door open, for she knew that it is a very silly thing to shut oneself into a wardrobe.) It seemed to be still daylight there. “I can always get back if anything goes wrong,” thought Lucy. She began to walk forward, *crunch-crunch*, over the snow and through the wood towards the other light.

Date ____________________

Name ____________________

Week 8
Day One

Narration Exercise

From *The Lion, the Witch and the Wardrobe* by C. S. Lewis

Date ____________________

Name ____________________

Dictation Exercise

From *The Lion, the Witch and the Wardrobe*

by C. S. Lewis

All four of the children have now gone through the wardrobe into the country Lucy has discovered: Narnia. There they meet two beavers who take them home to dinner. The oldest brother, Peter, and Mr. Beaver go fishing in the river, while the others help Mrs. Beaver get the rest of the meal ready.

"Gum boots" are rubber boots, and "oilskins" are like raincoats. A "marmalade roll" is a sweet cake with a jam filling.

Meanwhile the girls were helping Mrs. Beaver to fill the kettle and lay the table and cut the bread and put the plates in the oven to heat and draw a huge jug of beer for Mr. Beaver from a barrel which stood in one corner of the house, and to put on the frying pan and get the dripping hot. Lucy thought the Beavers had a very snug little home though it was not at all like Mr. Tumnus's cave. There were no books or pictures and instead of beds there were bunks, like on board ship, built into the wall. And there were hams and strings of onions hanging from the roof and against the walls were gum boots and oilskins and hatchets and pairs of shears and spades and trowels and things for carrying mortar in and fishing rods and fishing nets and sacks. And the cloth on the table tho' very clean was very rough.

Just as the frying pan was nicely hissing Peter and Mr. Beaver came in with the fish which Mr. Beaver had already opened with his knife and cleaned out in the open air. You can think how good the new-caught fish smelled while they were frying and how the hungry children longed for them to be done and how very much hungrier still they had become before Mrs. Beaver said, "Now we're nearly ready." Susan drained the potatoes and then put them all back in the empty pot to dry on the side of the range while Lucy was helping Mrs. Beaver to dish up the trout, so that in a very few minutes everyone was drawing up stools (it was all three-legged stools in the Beavers' house except for Mrs. Beaver's own special rocking chair beside the fire) and preparing to enjoy themselves. There was a jug of creamy milk for the children (Mr. Beaver stuck to beer) and a great big lump of deep yellow butter in the middle of the table from which everyone took as much as he wanted to go with his potatoes and all the children thought—and I agree with them—that there's nothing to beat good freshwater fish if you eat it when it has been alive half an hour ago and has come out of the pan half a minute ago. And when they had finished the fish Mrs. Beaver brought unexpectedly out of the oven a great and gloriously sticky marmalade roll, steaming hot, and at the same time moved the kettle on to the fire, so that when they had finished the marmalade roll the tea was made and ready to be poured out. And when each person had got his (or her) cup of tea, each person shoved back his (or her) stool so as to be able to lean against the wall and gave a long sigh of contentment.

Date ____________________

Name ______________________________________

Week 8
Day Three

Narration/Dictation Exercise

From *The Lion, the Witch and the Wardrobe* by C. S. Lewis

Date ____________________

Name ____________________

Dictation Exercise

Date ______________________

Name ______________________________________

Creative Writing

This page is left blank intentionally.

From *C. S. Lewis: The Man Behind Narnia*

by Beatrice Gormley

At the beginning of The Lion, the Witch and the Wardrobe*, the four children are sent away from London because the city is being bombed.* The Lion, the Witch and the Wardrobe *takes place during World War II. The author of the book, C. S. Lewis, knew what life during wartime was like. When he was a young man, he fought in World War I.*

This selection is from the biography C. S. Lewis: The Man Behind Narnia, *by Beatrice Gormley. (A biography is the true story of a real person's life.) In the biography, C. S. Lewis is called "Jack"—the name Lewis's friends and family used for him.*

When C. S. Lewis became a soldier, he was first sent to a training school called "officers' training corps." The "trenches" were deep, long ditches soldiers dug on the front lines of the battle. Soldiers stayed down inside the trenches for much of the fighting, since the trenches protected them from bullets fired by the other side. A "latrine" is an outhouse. (There were no warm comfortable bathrooms on the front lines of World War I!)

If you are not familiar with "enlisting" or "the draft," you should know that enlisting means joining the military, and that sometimes during wars governments required every healthy young man to join the military whether he wanted to or not. This was called "the draft." To be "exempt" from the draft meant that you would not be drafted, even if you were the right age.

While you are reading, you will see words inside brackets, like this: []. These show that extra words have been put into the original text to help you understand it better.

Since England was at war, every man over the age of eighteen was required to enlist for military service. Jack could have applied for an exemption from the draft, because his home residence was Ireland rather than England. To his father's distress, Jack refused to take the exemption. He was not at all enthusiastic about the war, but he felt it would be dishonorable not to serve.

During his spare time in the officers' training corps, perhaps spurred on by knowing that he might be killed in the war, Jack worked hard on a collection of poems. He intended to send it to a publisher.

On November 15 [1917], Jack heard alarming news: his battalion was ordered to the front lines of the war in France. They were given only two days' leave, not enough time for Jack to go home to Belfast and say goodbye....By November 29, his nineteenth birthday, Jack was in the trenches.

From there Jack wrote his father reassuring letters like this one:

This is a very quiet part of the line and the dug outs are much more comfortable than one imagines at home. They are very deep, you go down to them by a shaft of about twenty steps; they have wire bunks where a man can sleep quite snugly and brasiers [pans for holding burning coals] for warmth and cooking. Indeed, the chief discomfort is that they tend to get TOO hot, while the bad air makes one rather headachy. I had quite a pleasant time, and was only once in a situation of unusual danger, owing to a shell falling near the latrines while I was using them....

In his autobiography, Jack would describe a soldier's life on the front lines more vividly: "Through the winter, weariness and water were our chief enemies. I have gone to sleep marching and woken again and found myself marching still. One walked in the trenches in thigh gum boots with water above the knee; one remembers the icy stream welling up inside the boot when you punctured it on concealed barbed wire."

....On April 15, during the Battle of Arras in northern France, Second Lieutenant C. S. Lewis was wounded by an exploding artillery shell that killed his sergeant. Jack was taken to a mobile hospital in Etaples, on the coast of Normandy. There it was discovered that one of his wounds, caused by a piece of shrapnel lodged in his chest, was bad enough to put him out of combat permanently.

C. S. Lewis recovered from his wounds and went back to England, and back to his life as a reader and writer. The war ended in November 1918, a year after Lewis first went to fight in France.

Date ______________________________

Name ____

Week 9
Day One

Narration Exercise

From *C. S. Lewis: The Man Behind Narnia* by Beatrice Gormley

Date ______________________

Name ____

Week 9
Day Two

Dictation Exercise

From *Everyday Life: World War I*

by Walter A. Hazen

World War I, which took place when C. S. Lewis was a young man, began in 1914. Germany and its friends were known as the Central Powers; they were fighting against Great Britain, Russia, and France, who were called the Allies. The Germans were planning on invading France, and the Russians were planning on invading Germany. The French and British were afraid that the war would last a long time.

The selection below tells how differently the Germans and Russians felt.

"Kaiser" is the title that the Germans used for their king; "czar" is the Russian word for king. The Boulevard is a street in the French city of Paris.

Most wars begin amid much excitement and expectations of quick victory, and World War I was no exception. Every nation expected its warriors to be home safely by the onset of winter. This was especially true in Germany. The confident Germans gave the war no more than four months. Kaiser Wilhelm II told his departing troops that they would be home "before the leaves had fallen from the trees." One German officer went further, telling friends that he fully expected to be eating breakfast at one of Paris's more elegant cafes within a matter of weeks.

Departing German soldiers held similar views, scribbling boastful messages, such as "On to Paris" and "See you again on the Boulevard," on the sides of their transport trains as they departed for battle. They hung out the windows of the cars, waving and shouting as their trains pulled out of stations throughout Germany.

Not to be outdone, German civilians also got into the act. One famous picture of the time shows a young woman marching alongside the troops as they departed for the front. The same picture shows a man who had discarded his straw hat for a German soldier's helmet and marched along with the soldier's rifle on his shoulder.

Similar scenes took place throughout Europe. Huge crowds gathered in European capitals and cheered, sang, and danced. Young men rushed to recruitment offices to enlist. Some actually worried that the fighting would be over before they had a chance to fight. Others saw the war as an opportunity to escape from routine jobs. Few seemed to realize the horrors they would soon face.

Nowhere were expectations of success higher than in Russia. Russians were convinced that they would win and argued only about how long it would take. Most said two or three months, and anyone who suggested six months was thought to be an extreme pessimist. One Imperial Guard officer asked the czar's private physician if he should go ahead and pack his full-dress uniform so he would have it for the Russians' triumphal entry into Berlin [in Germany]. How's that for confidence?

Name

Date

Week 9
Day Three

Narration/Dictation Exercise

From *Everyday Life: World War I* by Walter A. Hazen

Date ______________________

Name ____

Week 9
Day Four

Dictation Exercise

Date ____________________

Name ____________________

Week 9
Day Five

Creative Writing

This page is left blank intentionally.

From *Farmer Boy*

by Laura Ingalls Wilder

Farmer Boy *tells the story of a young boy named Almanzo Wilder who lives on a farm in upstate New York in 1866. Almanzo is eight years old, and after school every day he has farm chores to do in the family's three big barns.*

You may have read the book Little House in the Big Woods, *which tells about Laura Ingalls Wilder's childhood. When Laura grew up, she married Almanzo Wilder.*

When Almanzo went into these great barns, he always went through into the Horse-Barn's little door. He loved horses. There they stood in their roomy box-stalls, clean and sleek and gleaming brown, with long black manes and tails. The wise, sedate work-horses placidly munched hay. The three-year-olds put their noses together across the bars; they seemed to whisper together. Then softly their nostrils whooshed along one another's necks; one pretended to bite, and they squealed and whirled and kicked in play. The old horses turned their heads and looked like grandmothers at the young ones. But the colts ran about excited, on their gangling legs, and stared and wondered.

They all knew Almanzo. Their ears pricked up and their eyes shone softly when they saw him. The three-year-olds came eagerly and thrust their heads out to nuzzle at him. Their noses, prickled with a few stiff hairs, were soft as velvet, and on their foreheads the short, fine hair was silky smooth. Their necks arched proudly, firm and round, and the black manes fell over them like a heavy fringe. You could run your hand along those firm, curved necks, in the warmth under the mane.

But Almanzo hardly dared to do it. He was not allowed to touch the beautiful three-year-olds. He could not go into their stalls, not even to clean them. He was only eight years old, and Father would not let him handle the young horses or the colts. Father didn't trust him yet, because colts and young, unbroken horses are very easily spoiled.

A boy who didn't know any better might scare a young horse, or tease it, or even strike it, and that would ruin it. It would learn to bite and kick and hate people, and then it would never be a good horse.

Almanzo did know better; he wouldn't ever scare or hurt one of those beautiful colts. He would always be quiet, and gentle, and patient; he wouldn't startle a colt, or shout at it, not even if it stepped on his foot. But Father wouldn't believe this.

So Almanzo could only look longingly at the eager three-year-olds. He just touched their velvety noses, and then he went quickly away from them, and put his barn frock over his good school-clothes.

Father had already watered all the stock, and he was beginning to give them their grain. Royal and Almanzo took pitchforks and went from stall to stall, cleaning out the soiled hay underfoot, and spreading fresh hay from the mangers to make clean beds for the cows and the oxen and the calves and the sheep.

They did not have to make beds for the hogs, because hogs make their own beds and keep them clean.

In the South Barn, Almanzo's own two little calves were in one stall. They came crowding each other at the bars when they saw him. Both calves were red, and one had a white spot on his forehead. Almanzo had named him Star. The other was a bright red all over, and Almanzo called him Bright.

Star and Bright were young calves, not yet a year old. Their little horns had only begun to grow hard in the soft hair by their ears. Almanzo scratched around the little horns, because calves like that. They pushed their moist blunt noses between the bars and licked with their rough tongues.

Date ____________________

Name ______________________________

Week 10
Day One

Narration Exercise

From *Farmer Boy* by Laura Ingalls Wilder

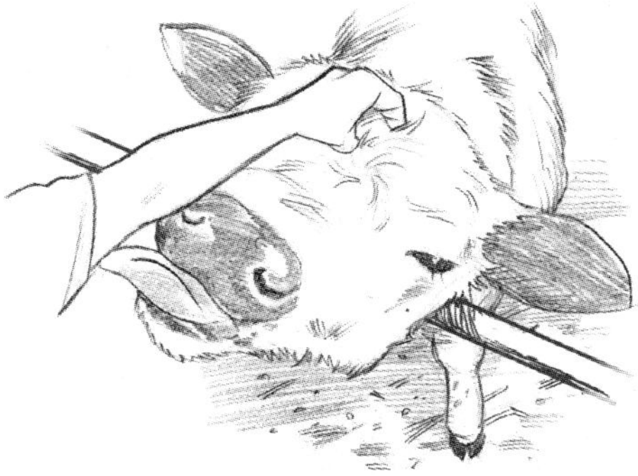

Date ______________________

Name ____

Week 10
Day Two

Dictation Exercise

From *Farmer Boy*

by Laura Ingalls Wilder

After chores, Almanzo and his brother Royal go into the house, where their mother and their sisters, Eliza Jane and Alice, have been getting dinner on the table. The schoolmaster, Mr. Corse, has come to dinner with the family.

You may not be familiar with some of the foods. "Headcheese" was made by cleaning the animal's head and boiling it until all of the remaining meat fell off. The bones were then taken out, and the liquid and bits of meat were poured into molds. This cooled and solidified, like Jello, because of the natural gelatin in the animal's meat and bones. Slices could then be cut off of it.

This may sound disgusting to you, but people have eaten headcheese since the Middle Ages. In fact, Susan (the author of this book) ate headcheese when she was little; her grandmother, who was a very traditional cook, made it on hog-killing days.

There were slabs of tempting cheese, there was a plate of quivering headcheese; there were glass dishes of jams and jellies and preserves, and a tall pitcher of milk, and a steaming pan of baked beans with a crisp bit of fat pork in the crumbling brown crust.

Almanzo looked at them all, and something twisted in his middle. He swallowed, and went slowly away.

The dining-room was pretty. There were green stripes and rows of tiny red flowers on the chocolate-brown wall-paper, and Mother had woven the rag-carpet to match. She had dyed the rags green and chocolate-brown, and woven them in stripes, with a tiny stripe of red and white rags twisted together between them. The tall corner cupboards were full of fascinating things—sea-shells, and petrified wood, and curious rocks, and books. And over the center-table hung an air-castle. Alice had made it of clean yellow wheat-straws, set together airily, with bits of bright-colored cloth at the corners. It swayed and quivered in the slightest breath of air, and the lamplight ran gleaming along the golden straws.

But to Almanzo the most beautiful sight was his mother, bringing in the big willow-ware platter full of sizzling ham.

Mother was short and plump and pretty. Her eyes were blue, and her brown hair was like a bird's smooth wings. A row of little red buttons ran down from the front of her dress of wine-colored wool, from her flat white linen collar to the white apron tied round her waist. Her big sleeves hung like large red bells at either end of the blue platter. She came through the doorway with a little pause and a tug, because her hoop-skirts were wider than the door.

The smell of ham was almost more than Almanzo could bear.

Mother set the platter on the table. She looked to see that everything was ready, and the table properly set. She took off her apron and hung it in the kitchen. She waited until Father had finished what he was saying to Mr. Corse. But at last she said,

"James, supper is ready."

It seemed a long time before they were all in their places. Father sat at the head of the table, Mother at the foot. Then they must all bow their heads while Father asked God to bless the food. After that, there was a little pause before Father unfolded his napkin and tucked it in the neckband of his frock.

He began to fill the plates. First he filled Mr. Corse's plate. Then Mother's. Then Royal's and Eliza Jane's and Alice's. Then, at last, he filled Almanzo's plate.

"Thank you," Almanzo said. Those were the only words he was allowed to speak at table. Children must be seen and not heard. Father and Mother and Mr. Corse could talk, but Royal and Eliza Jane and Alice and Almanzo must not say a word.

Almanzo ate the sweet, mellow baked beans. He ate the bit of salt pork that melted like cream in his mouth. He ate mealy boiled potatoes, with brown ham-gravy. He ate the ham. He bit deep into velvety bread spread with sleek butter, and he ate the crisp golden crust. He demolished a tall heap of pale mashed turnips, and a hill of stewed yellow pumpkin. Then he sighed, and tucked his napkin deeper into the neckband of his red waist. And he ate plum preserves, and strawberry jam, and grape jelly, and spiced watermelon-rind pickles. He felt very comfortable inside. Slowly he ate a large piece of pumpkin pie.

Date ____________________

Name ____

Week 10
Day Three

Narration/Dictation Exercise

From *Farmer Boy* by Laura Ingalls Wilder

Date ______________________

Name ____

Dictation Exercise

Date ____________________

Name ____________________

Week 10
Day Five

Creative Writing

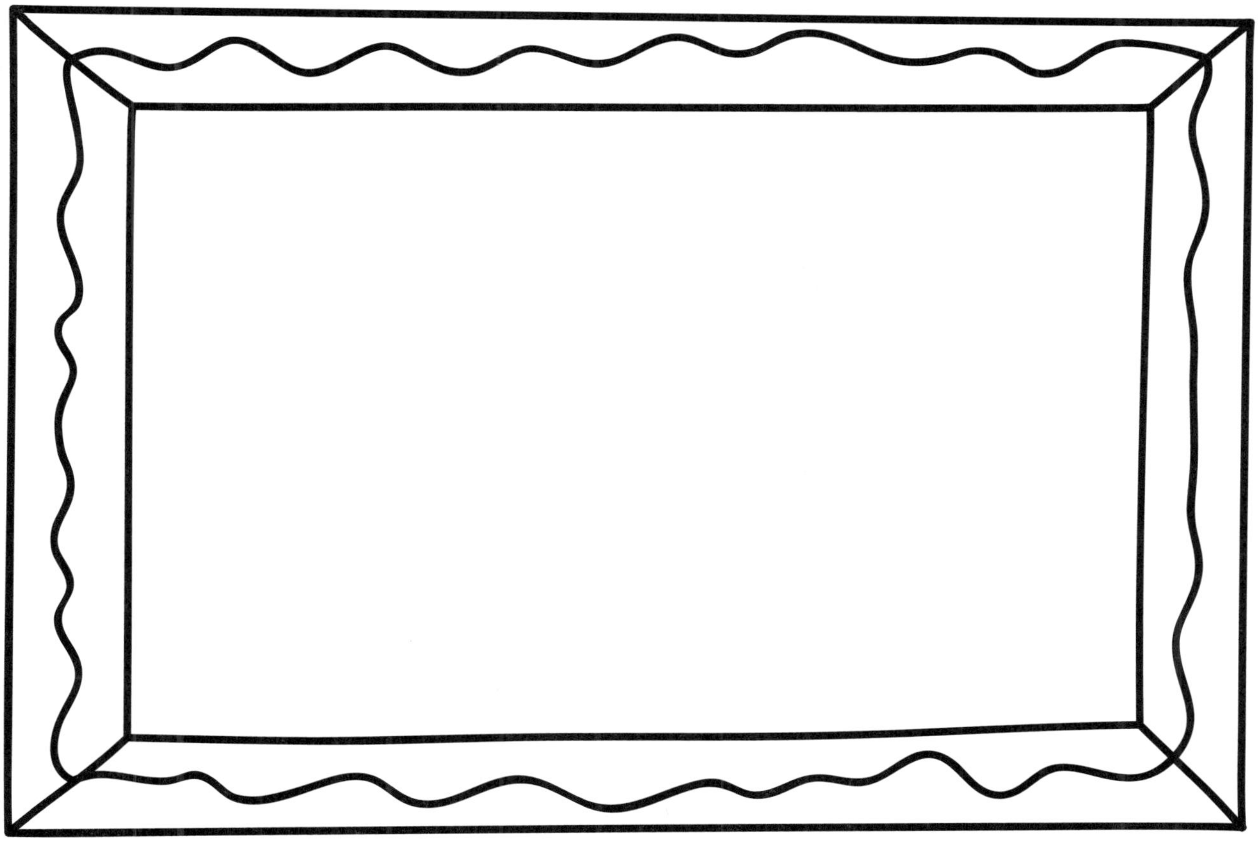

This page is left blank intentionally.

From *Tales of Ancient Egypt*

by Roger Lancelyn Green

This passage comes from the Egyptian story "The Treasure Thief." It is about the great Pharaoh Rameses III, who ruled Egypt around 1182–1151 BC. According to this story, Rameses asked his Master Builder, Hor-em-heb, to built him a pyramid that would keep not only his body, but his treasures, safe. But Hor-em-heb tricked him.

This story was first written down by the Greek historian Herodotus around 425 BC. An English writer named Roger Lancelyn Green took the Greek story and retold it in his book Tales of Ancient Egypt.

Under the care of the Master Builder the walls of the new building were reared and a pyramid was built over the whole, leaving a great treasure chamber in the middle. In the entrance he set sliding doors of stone, and others of iron and bronze; and when the untold riches of Pharaoh Rameses were placed in the chamber, the doors were locked and each was sealed with Pharaoh's great seal, that none might copy on pain of death....

Yet Hor-em-heb the Master Builder played Pharaoh false. In the thick wall of the Treasure House he made a narrow passage, with a stone at either end turning on a pivot that, when closed, looked and felt like any other part of the smooth, strong wall—except for those who knew where to feel for the hidden spring that held it firmly in place.

By means of this secret entrance Hor-em-heb was able to add to the reward which Pharaoh gave to him when the Treasure House was complete. Yet he did not add much, for very soon a great sickness fell upon him, and presently he died.

But on his death-bed he told his two sons about the secret entrance to the Treasure House; and when he was dead, and they had buried his body with all honour in a rock chamber among the Tombs of the Nobles at Western Thebes, the two young men made such good use of their knowledge that Pharaoh soon realized that his treasure was beginning to grow mysteriously less.

Rameses was at a loss to understand how the thieves got in, for the royal seals were never broken, but get in they certainly did. Pharaoh was fast becoming a miser, and he paid frequent visits to his Treasure House and knew every object of value in it—and the treasure continued to go.

At last Pharaoh commanded that cunning traps and meshes should be set near the chests and vessels from which the treasure was disappearing.

This was done secretly; and when next the two brothers made their way into the Treasure House by the secret entrance to collect more gold and jewels, the first to step across the floor towards the chests was caught in one of the traps and knew at once that he could not escape.

Date ____________________

Name ____________________

Week 11
Day One

Narration Exercise

From *Tales of Ancient Egypt* by Roger Lancelyn Green

Date ____________________

Name ____

Week 11
Day Two

Dictation Exercise

This page is left blank intentionally.

From *The Histories*

by Herodotus

trans. by Robin Waterfield

This is Herodotus' version of this same story about the Egyptian king Rameses. "Depredations" are "acts of robbing or plundering."

He wanted to store his money in a safe place, so he built a stone chamber as an extension off one of the outside walls of his residence. The builder, however, came up with the following crafty scheme. He cleverly fitted one of the stones in such a way that it would easily be removable from its wall by two men or even one. Anyway, the chamber was finished and the king stored his money in it. Time passed. At the end of his life, the builder summoned his sons (there were two of them) and told them of the plan he had put into effect while building the king's treasure-chamber, so that they would be comfortable for the rest of their lives. He explained precisely to them how to remove the stone and described its position in the wall. He told them that if they remembered his instructions, they would be the stewards of the king's treasury.

He died, and his sons soon set to work. They went by night to the royal residence and found the stone in the building. It was easy for them to handle, and they carried off a lot of money. When the king happened to go into the chamber next, he was surprised to see that the caskets were missing some money, but the seals on the door were still intact and the chamber had been locked up, so he could not blame anyone. But the same thing happened the next couple of times he opened the door as well: his money was obviously dwindling all the time (for the thieves had not stopped their depredations). So the king had traps made, and set them around the caskets which held the money. The thieves came as usual and one of them sneaked into the chamber, but as soon as he approached a casket he was caught in the trap.

Date ______________________

Name ____

Week 11
Day Three

Narration/Dictation Exercise

From *The Histories* by Herodotus

Date ____________________

Name ____________________

Week 11
Day Four

Dictation Exercise

Date ______________________

Name ____

Creative Writing

From "Ali Baba and the Forty Thieves"

by Jacob and Wilhelm Grimm

This story comes from an old collection of fairy tales called The Thousand and One Nights. *This version was retold by Jacob and Wilhelm Grimm.*

Once upon a time, in a distant Persian city, lived two brothers called Ali Baba and Kasim. Ali Baba was terribly poor, and he lived with his wife in a mud hut. He picked up sticks in the woods and sold them in bundles at the market.

Kasim, however, had a rich wife, and he lived in a big fine house and sold carpets. He became richer than ever. One day, as Ali Baba was gathering sticks in a wood some way from the city, he heard a band of horsemen gallop towards him. Scared that he might be in trouble for stealing wood, he scrambled up a tree and hid amongst the foliage, seconds before the men, armed to the teeth, rode underneath.

They were robbers, no doubt about that. Ali could tell by their evil looks, rough beards and bad language. But what made it perfectly clear to him was the booty they unloaded from their horses, obviously plundered in a raid. Their leader was a grim wicked-looking man. Followed by his men, he strode towards a rocky mountain nearby. Throwing wide his arms, he suddenly shouted, "Open Sesame!"

Ali Baba could hardly believe his eyes. For at the robber's words, the rock face swung open to become the entrance to a deep, dark cave. The robbers trooped inside, dragging their sacks. Ali Baba was struck dumb by this amazing sight, and he crouched in his tree, without moving a muscle. He could hear the robbers' voices echo in the cave, then out they came. Again opening his arms, the leader exclaimed loudly, "Close Sesame!" And the rock swung tightly shut, as they leapt onto their horses and galloped away.

Trembling with fear, Ali Baba climbed down the tree. He had just had the biggest shock of his life. Hardly aware of what he was doing, he muttered, "Open Sesame." But the mountain stood still.

Ali Baba said the words again, but this time he shouted them. Suddenly, the rock began to move. Ali Baba lit a flare and entered the cave. In front of his bulging eyes lay vast piles of treasure: pots of silver and gold, precious vases, weapons studded with rubies and emeralds, diamonds, carved plates and carpets, all heaped together.

The poverty-stricken stick-gatherer rubbed his eyes in disbelief. His hand was shaking like a leaf, as he picked up a gold coin.

"It's real!" he said in awe. Jabbering with excitement and stunned at the sight of such untold wealth, he told himself, "I'll take some coins. Nobody will ever know!" And he filled four bags full.

The second he reached home, Ali Baba locked the door and emptied the sacks in front of his astounded wife. "Count them," he ordered her triumphantly, before telling her what had happened. But there were far too many coins for these poor people to count.

"We can't count them all. Run to my brother's house and ask him for a corn measure. We'll use that," said Ali Baba.

When Kasim's wife heard this strange request, her curiosity was aroused. "I wonder what they want to measure," she thought. "It can't be corn, they're far too poor." And she quickly brushed a touch of tar across the bottom of the measuring pail. And when she got the pail back there was something stuck to it—as the clever woman had known there would be.

It was a gold coin.

Date ____________________

Name ____

Week 12
Day One

Narration Exercise

From "Ali Baba and the Forty Thieves" by the Brothers Grimm

Date ____________________

Name ____

Week 12
Day Two

Dictation Exercise

From "Ali Baba and the Forty Thieves"

by Jacob and Wilhelm Grimm

In this passage, the story of Ali Baba and his brother Kasim continues.

Kasim's wife was immediately filled with envy. "What!" she said. "How did Ali Baba get so much gold that he has to measure it? Where did he get all this wealth?"

Kasim, her husband, was at his shop. When he came home, his wife said to him: "Kasim, I know you think yourself rich, but Ali Baba is infinitely richer than you. He does not even count his money. He measures it." Then she told him how she had discovered Ali Baba's wealth, and showed him the piece of money, which was so old that they could not tell in what prince's reign it was coined.

Instead of being pleased at his brother's good fortune, Kasim became more and more jealous of Ali Baba's prosperity. He could not sleep all that night, and went to him in the morning before sunrise. "Ali Baba," he said, "I am surprised at you. You pretend to be miserably poor, and yet you measure gold. My wife found this at the bottom of the measure you borrowed yesterday."

Ali Baba realized that Kasim and his wife had discovered their secret. Knowing that he could not hide the wealth, he told Kasim all about the cave, and offered his brother part of his treasure to keep the secret.

Kasim rose the next morning long before the sun, and set out for the forest alone, with ten mules bearing ten great chests which he intended to fill. He followed the road which Ali Baba had told him about. It was not long before he reached the rocky mountain. When he reached the entrance of the cavern, he shouted, "Open, Sesame!"

The door immediately opened, and when he was in, closed upon him. He looked around the cave and saw rich bales of silk, embroideries, gold and silver in great heaps, and money in bags. He quickly laid as many bags of gold as he could carry at the door of the cavern; but his thoughts were so full of the great riches he should possess, that he could not think of the word to make it open. Instead of "Open, Sesame!" he said, "Open, Barley!" and was surprised to find that the door remained fast shut.

He named several sorts of grain, but still the door would not open. The more he tried to remember the word "Sesame," the more confused he became. Soon his memory had lost the word altogether, as if he had never heard it mentioned. He threw down the bags he had loaded himself with, and walked up and down the cave in great fear, without even looking at the riches around him.

Date ____________________

Name ____

Narration/Dictation Exercise

From "Ali Baba and the Forty Thieves" by the Brothers Grimm

Date ____________________

Name ____________________

Week 12
Day Four

Dictation Exercise

Date ____________________

Name ____

Week 12
Day Five

Creative Writing

From *The Four-Story Mistake*

by Elizabeth Enright

In The Four-Story Mistake, *the four Melendy children, their father, and their housekeeper, Cuffy, have just moved from New York City into a big house in the country. Although they were sad to leave their old house in the city, the new house is filled with secrets—and the country is filled with adventures.*

The youngest boy, Oliver, is exploring the house and has just discovered two doors, down in the basement. The "Cassidy children" are the children who lived in the house before the Melendy family bought it. "The Office" is what the Melendy children call their playroom. Its walls are covered with pictures of olden times.

From the furnace room two other chambers opened out. In the first one Oliver found an old bedspring, an empty barrel, and a Mason jar high up on the windowsill containing nothing but a large, hairy spider which he did not disturb. The spider's web was laced across the window, and was hung with dried fragments of moth wings, and the husks of beetles and houseflies.

The second room had a wooden door which was shut. Oliver had a hard time getting it open: it was stuck in its casing as though it had not been opened for a very long time. But he pushed against it with all his weight and finally it flew open and he flew into the room with it.

He could hardly believe his eyes.

This room was smaller than the other, and it was to Oliver as the cave was to Ali Baba: a storehouse full of treasure.

The first things he saw were two sleds propped up against the wall on their hind legs. They were very old, with rusted runners, and one was red, and one was blue. Names were painted on them in fancy letters. "Snow Demon," said one; and "Little Kriss Kringle," said the other. They must have belonged to the Cassidy children, thought Oliver. And then he saw the bicycle. Upstairs in the attic there were pictures of boys riding bicycles like this one. The front wheel was taller than he was, though the back wheel was small; and the saddle and handlebars soared loftily atop the front wheel. If only my legs were longer, thought Oliver, impatiently, looking down at his short, fat underpinnings; this bike is much better than the kind they have nowadays; more dangerous.

Besides the bicycle and the sleds, there was an old-fashioned tin bathtub covered with rust and chipped paint of robin's-egg blue, and shaped like an armchair with a high back. And there were more Mason jars, with more spiders in them, and a doll carriage made of decaying leather, and a broken coffee grinder, and a cast-iron crib frame, and a set of big books. All the objects in the room were covered with a layer of fine, ashy, white dust. Oliver sat down on one of the books, took another on his lap, reveling in the dust, and began to look at it. It turned out to be the bound volume of a magazine called *Harper's Young People,* published in the year 1887. The book was mildewed, some of its pages were glued together by years of damp, and its green cover had been gnawed by mice, but it exuded the indescribably delicious odor of all ancient books; better still, it was full of the pictures and adventures of the children of that other world which he had already explored on the walls of the Office upstairs. A world where girls wore sashes and long hair, and boys wore long stockings and button boots, and the horses which pulled the trolley cars wore straw hats. In that world there were no automobiles, no airplanes, no streamline trains, and yet the children seemed to be almost the same kind of children there were now.

Overhead Cuffy's feet creaked to and fro across the kitchen floor boards. Outside the morning was clear and golden with Indian summer. But Oliver sat in the dim light of his cellar room; pale and happy as a mushroom in its native habitat.

Date ______________________

Name ______________________

Week 13
Day One

Narration Exercise

From *The Four-Story Mistake* by Elizabeth Enright

Date ____________________

Name ____________________

Week 13
Day Two

Dictation Exercise

From *The Four-Story Mistake*

by Elizabeth Enright

Later in the year, the Melendy children experience their first snowstorm in the country. Oliver and his older brother, Rush, along with their two sisters, Mona and Randy, and their dog, Isaac, head out to try the sleds Oliver found in the cellar room.

The sleds turned out to be all right, though not greased lightning by any means. Rush had an inspiration, too, and went and got two large dishpans from the house; so each of them had a suitable vehicle for traveling down a snowy hill. The dishpans were particularly exciting, because they not only descended rapidly, but spun round and round while doing so. At the bottom of the slope you rose with difficulty, staggered, and discovered that you were the exact center of a world that revolved about you like a mammoth merry-go-round. Oliver was the only one who didn't care for this. His stomach resented the spinning of the dishpan, though for some reason it did not resent being slammed down belly-whopper on a sled over and over again....

"I know what let's do," Mona said, when they were all exhausted and hot and red-cheeked. "I read about it in a book. They made snow ice cream in this book. Why don't we make some?"

"How do we do it?"

"Well, first we have to beg a bottle of milk and some sugar from Cuffy. You do it, Rush. You're best at it."

"Okay," said Rush, who was hungry, trotting obediently toward the house.

"And some cups," called Mona, "and some spoons!"

Then she and Randy and Oliver went looking for the cleanest, purest patch of snow they could find, which was in the middle of the front lawn; untouched, unmarked, it looked as though it had been created to be eaten.

It tasted very good, too, though rather flat, later on when Rush had brought sugar and milk to mix with it. Oliver ate so much that his alert and responsive little stomach felt strange again, and he retired to the house.

Mona and Randy gathered up cups and spoons and went back to the house, too. But Rush left them and took a walk up into the woods. It was dusk, but the snow lent a strange radiance to the world. Flakes still fell, melting cold on his cheek, whispering with a feathery sound. There was no sound but their whisper, and his boots crunching softly. Isaac bounded at his heels with a white beard and ear-fringes.

"Just think," Rush said, "almost a year ago I found you. And in a snowstorm like this." He leaned down and patted Isaac, who looked up at him lovingly with one cold paw raised out of the snow. "Let's go back," Rush said. The woods were beautiful and mysterious; but suddenly he was cold; he longed for noise, and warmth and light. Isaac understood; he turned with a little yelp of joy and galloped beside his master down the hill toward the bright windows of the kitchen.

Date ______________________

Name ____

Narration/Dictation Exercise

From *The Four-Story Mistake* by Elizabeth Enright

Date ____________________

Week 13
Day Four

Name ____

Dictation Exercise

Date ____________________

Name ____________________

Creative Writing

This page is left blank intentionally.

From *The Moffats*

by Eleanor Estes

The four Moffat children live in a yellow house on Dollar Street. Sylvie, the oldest, is fifteen; Joey is twelve; Janey is nine; and the youngest, Rufus, is five and a half. Their cat Catherine has just had four kittens, and the children are getting ready to play a game that will help each one of them choose a kitten as a pet.

The children looked the kittens over and decided on temporary names for them. The little gray one they called Boots because of her truly extraordinary feet. Another kitten they named Mask. This one was black all over except for its face, which was white. It was Rufus who thought up the name Mask for it. Another they called Whiskers and the last one they named Funny because she had one green eye and one blue eye. Next Sylvie wrote each of these four names on four pieces of paper. These she dropped into Mama's hat.

"Now, who will be the one to draw out the names?" Sylvie asked.

"Rufus! Rufus!" cried Joe and Janey. "Because he is the littlest."

"All right," said Sylvie. "Whichever cat has his name drawn by Rufus will be set in the middle of the room. Then we will all go to the four corners of the room and call, Kitty, Kitty. Whichever person that kitten goes to, why, that person will be the winner of that kitten."

Sylvie had thought this game up years ago and they all loved it.

So now Rufus closed his eyes, put his chubby fist into the hat, and drew out the first name. They waited with bated breath while Sylvie read the name.

"Funny!" she said.

A cheer went up as Funny was put in the middle of the room.

"Kitty, kitty, kitty," the children called from the four corners of the room. In this game it was possible that you might have a preference for one or another of the four kittens. But this must never be evident. You must call as fervently for this one as that one.

"Kitty, kitty, kitty," they called to the little one named Funny.

"Muu-u-r-r." A very feeble, wistful cry came from Funny. She turned around with difficulty. She was feeling terribly alone in a strange world. Suddenly she rushed as fast as she could towards Jane. However, walking in a straight line was utterly impossible for her and it was Sylvie's corner she finally ended up in. So Sylvie and Funny were out of the game.

Rufus scrunched up his face, put his hand in the hat again. The name was—Whiskers!

Whiskers! Cheers again. But Whiskers didn't care. He just sat there with his head nodding on his shoulders, looking as though he were going to fall asleep at any moment.

"Kitty, kitty, kitty," Joe, Jane, and Rufus coaxed.

Whiskers just sat there and looked around the room with a pleasant though simple expression.

"Come, Whiskers. Come, kitty," they pleaded again.

But Whiskers just sat there, swaying gently to and fro.

"We shall have to go nearer this one," said Joey in the manner of a patient parent.

Joey, Jane, and Rufus drew nearer, to within a few feet of Whiskers. Still he just sat.

"He doesn't want to play," said Rufus in disgust.

Now the three went right up close to him. Just a kitten's length away. At this, Whiskers stood up on his shaky legs and staggered nonchalantly over to Rufus. He nestled comfortably on his sleeve and was asleep in a second. So Rufus and Whiskers were out of the game too.

Date ______________________

Name ______________________

Week 14
Day One

Narration Exercise

From *The Moffats* by Eleanor Estes

Date ______________________

Name ____

Week 14
Day Two

Dictation Exercise

From *The Moffats*

by Eleanor Estes

Boots, a gray kitten who springs happily around on enormous feet, is Jane's favorite kitten, and Jane is desperate to get her. But Jane thinks to herself that she really doesn't deserve Boots. She is feeling guilty because a neighbor gave her money to buy candy earlier in the day, and instead of sharing the money with her sister and brothers, Jane bought herself an ice-cream cone and ate the whole thing herself.

Now just Boots and Mask were left. And Joe and Jane.

"Oh, please let Boots be mine," Jane prayed again and again. "Although of course I know I don't deserve it," she added.

Rufus drew again. This time the name was—Boots.

Boots! The children all cheered lustily. Boots herself seemed full of excitement. All the while the game had been going on, she had been clawing at the soap box and miaowing madly to get out. Now she was out!

"Oh, be mine, be mine," breathed Jane.

"Look at the big toes on her," Joe marveled. "Boy, oh, boy, I hope I win her."

Of course Joe was just as anxious for Boots as Jane was. And why shouldn't he be? Of these four sweet kittens she alone showed marks of personality that lifted her above the usual run of cats and kittens. She paid no attention to Joe or to Jane. Instead she raced madly around the room. She whacked at a tassel that was hanging from the red plush chair. This caused her to lose her balance and she rolled over and over. Up again. She resumed her swift, though wobbly, adventuring through the sitting-room, the new world.

"Oh, pussy, come. Come, pussy," Jane begged.

Boots ran right over to Jane's corner but then, just as she was within a cat's length of her, she backed off to the middle of the room. What a kitten!

"Come, kitty, come, kitty," said Joey in that gentle voice of his that surely Boots would not be able to resist.

Now Boots teetered over towards Joe. She sat down not far from him and stared at him with her big blue eyes. Her little pink tongue was hanging out and she was thoroughly irresistable. Suddenly she began to purr. She was the first one to purr and she sounded like a little engine.

"She's going to Joey," mourned Jane. "Well, of course I don't deserve her."

But at this moment Boots suddenly turned right about again. She jumped wildly into the air a couple of times and then, in a series of little sideways leaps, she landed right in Jane's lap. Tears came into Jane's eyes. "She's mine. She's mine," she cried, burying her nose in Boots' sweet-smelling fur.

So Mask went to Joey and he immediately found many engaging things about this kitten that they had not yet discovered. For instance, he had the longest fur, the prettiest markings, the longest tail, and many other unusual qualities. Moreover he was the smallest of the four and would need special attention.

At this moment Catherine-the-cat came in. She looked around the room disdainfully. Then she jumped into the soap-box and whirrupped for her kittens. Jane gave Boots one last hug. She already loved this little kitten so much it was almost more than she could bear. She put the kitten carefully back into the soap-box as the other children were doing with theirs. And the choosing game was over.

Date ______________________

Name ______________________

Narration/Dictation Exercise

From *The Moffats* by Eleanor Estes

Date ____________________

Name ____

Week 14
Day Four

Dictation Exercise

Date ____________________

Name ____

Creative Writing

Names:

____

____

____

This page is left blank intentionally.

From *The Lemonade Trick*

by Scott Corbett

Kerby has a mysterious chemistry set. It was given to him by a strange old lady named Mrs. Graymalkin. He's not sure what the chemicals do—but he decides to try out an experiment, just for fun.

Waldo is Kerby's dog. Dr. Jekyll and Mr. Hyde *is a famous book by Robert Louis Stevenson.*

Kerby took a beaker to the bathroom and filled it half full of water. Returning to his room, he placed it in a wire stand that came with the set. Next he opened the same tube again and thrust an eyedropper into it. Holding the eyedropper and tube high where he could watch closely, he carefully pulled a tiny amount of liquid into the eyedropper.

Kerby felt very scientific.

"That ought to be about two drops," he said to Waldo, forgetting that Waldo had left.

He turned to the beaker half full of water. Carefully, holding his breath, he squeezed the chemical into the water.

Nothing happened.

No bubbling.

No boiling.

No steaming.

The water just sat there doing nothing. It was very disappointing. Kerby flopped down on his bed with an angry bounce.

"Aw heck! Might know her old chemistry set would be a fake!" he muttered, thinking hard thoughts about Mrs. Graymalkin.

After brooding for a moment, he sighed and decided to empty the beaker in the bathroom. After that he would try a couple of the other tricks, just to see if any of them would work. Probably the chemicals were old and had lost all their fizz, but maybe some of them were still good. He might as well try. While he was experimenting with the chemistry stuff, he could think of some excuse for not mowing the lawn.

As he walked down the hall he held the water up to the strong light pouring through the window at the end of the hall. The water was clear and not smoking or bubbling or boiling or steaming even a little bit. He sniffed it to see if the chemical gave it any smell.

Kerby stopped. The water had a strangely delightful, irresistibly tempting scent. Before he knew what he was doing, he obeyed a powerful urge.

He lifted the beaker to his lips and drank its contents.

The instant he did this, Kerby was scared.

He remembered all about *Dr. Jekyll and Mr. Hyde*, and what had happened to Dr. Jekyll when he got to messing around with *his* chemistry set. Dr. Jekyll had drunk some stuff he mixed up, and the next thing he knew he had changed into a horrible, hairy man who went out and did all sorts of terrible things. It made him bad, very bad.

With a scared cry, Kerby rushed into the bathroom and looked at himself in the mirror. Would he change into a monster before his very own eyes? Would his face get all hairy and his teeth turn into great fangs?

Date ____________________

Name ____

Week 15
Day One

Narration Exercise

From *The Lemonade Trick* by Scott Corbett

Date ____________________

Name ____________________

Week 15
Day Two

Dictation Exercise

From *The Lemonade Trick*

by Scott Corbett

This is the story of Kerby's experiment, continued. It begins with what happens right after he drinks the good-smelling water.

Then all at once his eyes rolled in circles, twice, and a strange feeling overcame him.

He felt good.

That was the only way to describe it. Good. Very good.

When Waldo had heard Kerby's scared cry, he must have thought his master was really in trouble, because he came running loyally to see what was the matter.

By the time he arrived that good feeling had come over Kerby. He was rinsing out the beaker and drying it on a paper towel. Waldo stared up at him inquiringly. Kerby gave him a kind and affectionate smile. He stooped and patted his best friend gently on the head.

"Waldo, I want to apologize for dragging you down the hall by the tail," he said. "That is a mean thing to do, and I won't do it again. Besides, your nails scratch Mom's floors. In fact, they may already have done so from time to time. Later on I must remember to polish the floors for her."

Waldo reared back and gave his master a worried look. Kerby threw the paper towel in the wastebasket, being careful to see that it dropped in and did not litter up the bathroom floor. Then he returned to his room, with Waldo padding after him.

"I must put away my chemistry set now and not try any more experiments with it up here in my room," he told Waldo as he put away the beaker and closed the box. "After all, this is no place to play with chemicals—I might spill some and mark my furniture. Why, I didn't even spread any newspapers on my desk before I started! Besides, this is no time to be fooling around playing. I have work to do."

So saying, Kerby went outside and finished mowing the lawn. After he had finished mowing, he trimmed the grass around the trees and along the back fence. Then he raked up all the grass and put it on the compost heap.

When his mother came home, she found him down in the cellar finishing up his cleaning job there.

"What a wonderful job you did on the lawn!" she said, coming downstairs to stare at him in amazement. "I never saw such a job!"

"I was glad to do it, Mom," said Kerby.

"And now, to find you working down here—Kerby, do you feel all right?"

"I feel good, Mom," he said. "Very good."

“Well…” His mother still looked doubtful, but she rose and started upstairs. “I’ll fix some lunch, and—”

“It’s already fixed, Mom,” said Kerby, causing his mother to stumble on a step and nearly fall on her face, she was so surprised. “I thought I’d have it all ready for you when you came home.”

After lunch he worked in the basement again all afternoon. Every once in a while his mother called down in an anxious tone to make sure he was all right. Around three o-clock she even telephoned his father and had a long conversation in a low voice with him.

Date ____________________

Name ____

Narration/Dictation Exercise

From *The Lemonade Trick* by Scott Corbett

Date ______________________

Name ____

Week 15
Day Four

Dictation Exercise

Date ______________________

Name ______________________________________

Creative Writing

This page is left blank intentionally.

From *Magic...Naturally! Science Entertainments and Amusements*
by Vicki Cobb

Last week you read about a chemistry set that does real magic. Today, you're going to read about a "magic trick" done through chemistry. The trick: you place a coin in a dish, cover it with water, and then announce that you're going to get it out without wetting your fingers, using only a match, a birthday candle, and a glass.

YOU WILL NEED
- a small piece of clay to act as a candleholder
- a birthday candle
- a coin
- a shallow dish (such as a glass pie plate)
- water
- red or blue food coloring
- matches
- an 8-ounce glass or small glass jar

You can set this trick up right in front of your audience. Make a candleholder out of clay and place the candle in it.

Place the coin in the dish and pour in enough water to completely cover the coin. Add a few drops of food coloring to make the water more visible. Challenge anyone to remove the coin without tilting the dish, pouring out the water, or using an instrument to touch the coin—and without getting wet fingers.

When your audience has run out of ideas, announce that you will accomplish this feat with the aid of a candle, a match, and a glass. Place the candle in its holder in the dish as far from the coin as possible. Light the candle. Cover the lit candle with the glass. When the candle goes out (having used up all the oxygen in the glass) the water will be pushed by air pressure up into the glass (where there is a partial vacuum). The dish is now dry and you simply reach in and pick up the coin.

Here's how it works: If you empty a pail of water onto the floor, the water quickly spreads, flowing into even the smallest cracks in the floor. Air also flows into spaces not already occupied by air. The sound you hear when you open a vacuum-packed jar of coffee or peanuts is made by air rushing in as the seal is broken. The motor of a vacuum cleaner creates a partial vacuum in the bag. As air rushes in to fill this space, it sweeps up solid material in its path.

In this trick you create a partial vacuum by burning a candle in a closed space. When a candle burns it uses oxygen, which makes up about 20 percent of the gases in the air. (Most of the rest of air is another gas called nitrogen.) The flame goes out when all the oxygen has been used. The pressure of the air left in this closed space is less than the pressure outside. The water you want to remove from the coin is between this partial vacuum and the outside air. Like dirt being swept into a vacuum cleaner, the water can be pushed up into the closed spacc by the pressure of outside air.

Date ____________________

Name ____________________

Week 16
Day One

Narration Exercise

From *Magic...Naturally!* by Vicki Cobb

Date ______________________

Name ____

Week 16
Day Two

Dictation Exercise

Adapted from *Magic Through Science*

by Robert Gardner

The "magic" trick that you read about earlier this week was actually a scientific experiment. Other magic tricks are done by deceiving the audience. This is one example of a way that magicians often deceive their audience.

Tell your audience that you can read minds! Ask someone to volunteer to help you. After you have chosen your volunteer, tell the audience that you will leave the room. While you are gone, the audience will choose an object. When you return to the room, your volunteer will then point to different objects in the room. You will read the volunteer's mind, and choose the correct object.

When you return, the volunteer points to several objects. None of these are the objects selected, so each time, you answer, "That's not it." Then the volunteer points to the object selected by the audience. You say, "I can read your mind. That is the correct object!"

Explanation: Your volunteer is actually your partner. Ahead of time, select your volunteer and tell him or her that you need to establish a set of signals. The correct object will be the object which the volunteer points to right after pointing to something *red.* If the object *is* something red, you need an additional signal. Tell the volunteer that he or she should use the *right* hand for pointing—*unless* the selected object is red. If the selected object is red, the volunteer will use his or her *left* hand to point. The volunteer will also point to a *black* object right before pointing to the correct object.

Practice this together a number of times, until you can always identify the correct object. Then, make sure that you choose your partner from the volunteers at the magic show! Most "mind reading" tricks in magic shows involve a volunteer who is actually a partner of the magician.

Date ____________________

Name ______________________________________

Week 16
Day Three

Narration/Dictation Exercise

From *Magic Through Science* by Robert Gardner

Date ____________________

Name ____________________

Week 16
Day Four

Dictation Exercise

Date ______________________

Name ____

Week 16
Day Five

Creative Writing

From *Harry Houdini, Young Magician*

by Kathryn Kilby Borland

Harry Houdini was a famous magician who tricked his audience into believing that he had special powers. This selection is from a book about Houdini's childhood. Houdini's real name was Ehrich Weiss. Later, he changed his name to Harry Houdini because he thought it would sound better on stage.

In this story, young Houdini sees his very first magic trick—a man at a fair picks coins out of the air and fills a bucket with them. Houdini's family is very poor, so Houdini watches the man all day. He wants to learn how to make a bucket full of money so that he can take it home to his mother and father.

"Hey, kid!" the magician said, "why don't you go home like everybody else? You make me nervous watching, watching all day."

Ehrich looked around. It was true. He was the only one watching now. "I'm sorry, sir," he said. "I didn't think you'd notice me. It's just that I need to know how to fill the bucket with money, and I don't think I can quite do it yet. Could you—" Ehrich hesitated. The magician had sounded pretty cross.

The magician stared at him. "Are you pulling my leg, kid? Do you think I really pull money out of the air?"

"You don't really?" Ehrich asked. He was so pleased that the magician was actually talking to him that he almost forgot to be disappointed about not taking a bucket of money home. "Then where did it come from?"

Suddenly the magician smiled. "Look here, kid," he said. "I'm going to show you something. It's not what you really do in this business that counts. It's what people think you do. Now, when I show the empty bucket I hold it in my left hand, see? And in my left hand I also have a bunch of coins that nobody sees. They're too busy looking at the empty bucket. Now, in my right hand I have just one coin. See?"

Ehrich nodded. "But I saw you pick the coins out of the air."

"Aha! That's what you thought you saw. Here's what you really saw."

The man showed Ehrich that he was holding the coin behind his hand between his thumb and first finger. When he held his hand up, the coin did not show at all. Then he moved his fingers quickly. Now the coin could be plainly seen. Even though Ehrich saw him do the trick, it was hard to believe the man hadn't picked that coin out of the air.

"But how do you get another one after you throw that one in the bucket?"

"I don't throw it in."

"But I saw you do it every time."

"You thought you saw me. I acted as if I was throwing it in, but I slipped it in back of my hand again. At the same time I slipped a coin into the bucket out of my other hand. See how it's done? Come on up and try it."

"I don't think I could." But Ehrich's fingers were itching to try. He'd forgotten everything except the magician, the bucket, and the coins.

The first time he tried it the coins in his left hand fell to the floor. It was a hot day, and the coin in his right hand stuck between his fingers. He made every kind of mistake, but at last the magician said, "You're not doing badly, kid. You've got the fingers for it."

Date ______________________

Name ____

Week 17
Day One

Narration Exercise

From *Harry Houdini, Young Magician* by Kathryn Kilby Borland

Date

Name

Week 17
Day Two

Dictation Exercise

From *Harry Houdini*

by Rita Thievon Mullin

When he began doing magic in front of audiences, Houdini often escaped from handcuffs. He grew expert at picking locks with tiny pieces of metal or hidden keys which he would conceal in his clothing. But soon he wanted to add a new challenge to his act. This excerpt from the biography Harry Houdini *by Rita Thievon Mullin tells how he escaped from wooden boxes.*

As Harry continued to welcome handcuff challenges, he added a new element: the box challenge. In city after city, local carpenters would build more and more elaborate packing boxes from which the great Houdini would escape. Often the box would be displayed in the theater lobby for days before a big performance so that audiences could see how sturdy it was.

After the box was carried on stage, Houdini would be handcuffed, chained, and lifted into the box. The carpenters would put the top on the box and seal it shut with plenty of nails. Then the tall drapery cabinet would be placed around it to hide what was happening inside from the audience. The theater band played faster and louder with each passing minute, as Houdini worked to escape first from his bonds and then from the box. When he emerged from the cabinet and the drapery was opened, the box stood there, just as it had, with all the sides—and all the nails that had sealed it—still in place.

So amazing were his feats that some people in Europe claimed Houdini had supernatural powers. Houdini was always quick to say that his skills were all based in the natural world. In the case of his many box escapes, the trick was simple: Before the performance Harry and [his assistant] Franz would replace the long nails holding one side of the box with shorter nails that Harry could easily push out from the inside. Then, once Houdini was out, he could tap the long ones back in while the band played louder and faster.

As the box challenge became more popular, Houdini developed new ways to amaze audiences. Sometimes the box was actually built onstage in front of the audience, so substituting short "dummy nails" was impossible. In that case, Houdini might use a simple steel jack that worked like the ones used to raise a car for changing a tire. He would hide the parts of the jack in his clothing and assemble them after he was sealed in the box. The jack would apply pressure to one side of the box until the nails slipped out. After he was outside, he would take the jack apart again, hide the parts, and tap the nails back in place while the house band played the ear-blasting "Storm King" for the audience to hide the noise.

During the nearly five years Harry and [his wife] Bess traveled through Europe, they became the most popular vaudeville performers there. They played to packed houses and received reviews in newspapers that any performer would envy. Although they had made two trips back to the U.S. to visit family during their time in Europe, by 1905 they were homesick and ready to move back to take on American vaudeville....

On the new tour, Harry expanded the box challenge that had been so popular in Europe. This time, he invited people to dare him to escape from just about anything. The challengers were very creative! During his tour he escaped from the world's largest envelope (without tearing the paper), a clear-glass box, a coffin with the top screwed down, a man-sized sausage skin, and a giant-sized football carried onstage by the University of Pennsylvania football team.

Date ____________________________

Name ____

Narration/Dictation Exercise

From *Harry Houdini* by Rita Thievon Mullin

Date ______________________

Name ____

Week 17
Day Four

Dictation Exercise

Date ______________________

Name ____

Week 17
Day Five

Creative Writing

I ran to the bathroom and looked in the mirror. Nobody stood in the reflection. "The potion worked," I exclaimed. "I'm invisible!" I knew just what to do next . . .

This page is left blank intentionally.

From *Paul Bunyan Swings His Axe*

by Dell J. McCormick

Paul Bunyan is a legendary woodsman who is said to have been born in the woods of Maine. When he was grown, he was a giant of a man. He went west with a crew of lumberjacks to open his own logging camp. He took two cooks, nicknamed Hot Biscuit Slim and Cream Puff Fatty, with him. Stories say that everything Paul Bunyan owned was big—including his logging camp.

The Red River Valley stretches from the northern United States (North Dakota and Minnesota) into the Canadian territory of Manitoba.

When Paul moved his camp into the Red River country, he found that the dining room was too small to hold all his men. The kitchen was too small, too. Every day dinner would be from two to three hours late.

One day Paul got angry when dinner was late and shouted, "Hot Biscuit Slim, come here!"

Three men who were standing beside Paul were blown over by the force of his voice. They rolled over and over and landed on their feet. They started running and did not stop until they were well out of the reach of his voice.

Hot Biscuit Slim came on the run, and Paul said to him, "Slim, I want a larger kitchen where two hundred cooks can work at the same time. Also build a larger dining room. Make the tables six miles long! Yesterday the men sat down, and by the time the biscuits got there, they were cold. Nobody wants to eat cold biscuits!"

Slim had the men clear the forest for miles around and build a huge kitchen and dining room. Ole, the blacksmith, made a huge black kettle that held eleven hundred gallons of soup.

When Hot Biscuit Slim made soup, he rowed in the boiling water to the center of the big kettle with boatloads of cabbages, turnips, and potatoes. He shoveled the vegetables into the water, and in a few hours a wonderful soup was ready.

Ole also made a ten-acre hot-cake griddle. To grease the griddle, Hot Biscuit Slim strapped flat sides of bacon on the feet of the cookhouse boys and told them to skate back and forth over the huge griddle.

The boys had fun playing tag and crack-the-whip on the hot griddle. Sometimes they fell off and burned their trousers. When that griddle began to steam, no one could see across it because the fog was so thick.

For Sunday morning breakfast Hot Biscuit Slim tried to make his finest hot cakes. They were so large that it took five men to eat one. Paul himself often ate twelve to fourteen of the big cakes. The cookhouse boys worked all day Saturday mixing dough and bringing in huge barrels of maple syrup for the hot cakes.

The biggest meal of the week was Sunday dinner. Hot Biscuit Slim would cook the very best soup, the finest vegetables, and the nicest spring chicken of all for this meal.

One Saturday Slim said to Ole, "Tomorrow I am going to have the best Sunday dinner of the year. When the men are through eating my hot biscuits with jelly, my spinach, cucumbers, young red radishes, and my chicken pie, they won't be able to eat a mouthful of dessert."

Cream Puff Fatty overhead this big talk, and his pride was hurt. He made the desserts, and he thought such talk was running down his good name.

He said to himself, "So Hot Biscuit Slim thinks the boys won't eat any dessert? Well, we'll see about that."

Cream Puff Fatty called the dessert boys together and said, "We will make cream puffs that will melt in their mouths. Light creamy ones with whipped cream a foot high! We'll see if they refuse to eat dessert."

The Sunday dinner hour arrived, and then men sat down to eat. Soup, vegetables, and salads disappeared, and the men were almost full. Then they saw the chicken pie coming.

"Oh, look! Chicken pie!" they shouted. They knew Slim's chicken pie was the finest in the world, and they had to make room for it. The cookhouse boys on roller skates kept right on bringing in large platters of food.

"Hot biscuits and jelly! Hurrah!" the men cried, although they didn't seem to have room for another mouthful.

Cream Puff Fatty was in despair. He looked down the long dining room and saw that the men were slower and slower in lifting the food to their mouths. It looked as though they couldn't eat another bite.

"It's now or never, boys!" cried Cream Puff Fatty. The dessert boys had their roller skates strapped on, and they started down the long tables.

The men saw them coming and cried out, "Cream puffs! Cream puffs!" They started reaching for the fluffy white cakes piled full of rich custard cream. Not a man left the dining room until every cream puff was eaten.

Date ______________________

Name ____

Week 18
Day One

Narration Exercise

From *Paul Bunyan Swings His Axe* by Dell J. McCormick

Date ______________________________

Name ____

Week 18
Day Two

Dictation Exercise

From *The Story of Canada*

by Janet Lunn and Christopher Moore

It took many pairs of hands to cut and haul trees. Many newcomers to North America, immigrants from other countries, went to the lumber camps to find work. This selection from The Story of Canada *describes life in the lumber camps.*

Immigrants poured into British Canada like a flood. Sometimes ten thousand landed in a single week. Families laboured to clear the forests and plant new farms, to build up the cities and towns. Gangs of young men known as "navvies" slaved to cut canals around the rapids and waterfalls. They hauled timber from the Canadian woods, salted down codfish in Newfoundland, and launched trim sailing ships from Atlantic Canada's shipyards.

Most of the immigrants came from Britain. There were Scottish highlanders, driven from their glens by cruel landlords who wanted the land to raise sheep.... Families also came from overcrowded Ireland, or to escape teeming cities in England. They settled all over British America....The newcomers called British North America "a good poor man's country," meaning that anyone willing to work hard could do well. "In England there is too many men. Here there is not enough," wrote one young man in a letter to his family.

....Winter meant woodcutting. Men tramped off to timber shanties in the pine forests. They lived on pork and beans, swinging their broadaxes and hauling the timber over the snow to the riverbanks. When the spring runoff swelled the rivers, the lumberjacks became *draveurs*, or raftsmen, riding the logs down the rapids to the sawmills and timber ships. Only the strongest stayed with it: men like Joseph Montferrand.

For thirty years of the early 1800s, Montferrand was the greatest lumberjack on the Ottawa River. People said he was so strong that no boxer could beat him, so agile that he could plant his bootmarks on a tavern ceiling and land on his feet. He was a legend, maybe the most famous man in French Canada.

The lumber camps of the Ottawa Valley were rough and rowdy places. Montferrand led French-Canadian loggers in battles against the Irish loggers. Yet even his English-speaking rivals bragged that "Joe Mufferaw" could drink a lake dry, dig out a river channel by dragging his axe, and comb his hair with a tall pine tree. Wherever lumberjacks went in the north woods, they spread his name and fame.

Date ____________________

Name ____

Narration/Dictation Exercise

From *The Story of Canada* by Janet Lunn and Christopher Moore

Date

Name

Week 18
Day Four

Dictation Exercise

Date ______________________

Name ______________________

Week 18
Day Five

Creative Writing

From *The Story of the Declaration of Independence*

by Norman Richards

This excerpt from The Story of the Declaration of Independence *tells the story of the British colonies in North America, from their beginnings in 1620 up to the decision by those colonies in 1776 to rebel. The Continental Congress was a gathering of the colony leaders, who met together in Philadelphia to decide whether or not they would remain loyal to the British king.*

"Absolute rule" means that a king has power over every part of his subjects' lives—and the subject has no choice but to submit.

Ever since the Pilgrims had signed the Mayflower Compact, Americans had believed that absolute rule was wrong. In Europe kings ruled whether the people wanted them or not. Kings believed that it was their divine right to rule.

Americans had been living as free men, making their own laws for one hundred and fifty years. They would never surrender this precious freedom.

Richard Henry Lee of Virginia said in the Continental Congress: "These United Colonies are, and of right ought to be, free and independent states."

The members of the Continental Congress saw now that it was their duty to follow the people's wishes and declare the American colonies independent. They wanted officially to tell the world about the new union of the thirteen United States of America. They also wanted to tell the world why they were breaking away from Great Britain. Five men were chosen to work on the document—John Adams, Thomas Jefferson, Benjamin Franklin, Robert Livingston and Roger Sherman.

They chose young Thomas Jefferson from Virginia to write this official declaration. He was a smart man, and he could express ideas clearly. And they wanted this declaration understood by everybody.

Thomas Jefferson worked for two weeks writing the declaration. He stood at a desk in the second-floor parlor of a house belonging to a Philadelphia bricklayer whom he knew. He wrote on large paper with a quill (a feather) dipped in ink. He would study the sentences he had written the day before. If he didn't like them he would cross them out and write them again.

Jefferson, with four other men, was to present the declaration to the members of Congress. When he had finished writing the declaration he showed it to John Adams, Benjamin Franklin and the other members of the committee, and they made a few changes.

The Declaration of Independence has two main parts. The first part explains the beliefs of Americans about democracy. It tells that men have certain rights that can't be taken away from them. The signers declared these...truths to be understood by everyone: that all men are created equal; that all men are born with rights that no one can take away from them; that some of these rights are life, liberty, and the right to try to be happy; that the purpose of a government is to preserve these rights for all men....

The second part of the Declaration of Independence tells how the king refused to grant these rights to Americans. It contains a long list of examples of tyranny by the king. It tells the world why the colonies broke away from his rule and became the United States of America.

This document was presented to the members of the Congress. They debated about it for almost three days. It was approved on July 4, 1776, although the New York delegates did not accept it until eleven days later.

Date ____________________

Name ____________________

Week 19
Day One

Narration Exercise

From *The Story of the Declaration of Independence* by Norman Richards

Date ______________________

Name ____

Week 19
Day Two

Dictation Exercise

From *The Young Oxford History of Britain & Ireland*

by Mike Corbishley and Kenneth O. Morgan

The Declaration of Independence was not the first document to tell a king that his subjects have rights. Five hundred years earlier, the people of England had forced their king, King John, to sign a document that spelled out their rights. King John had been fighting a war against France, and he had been forcing his people to pay higher and higher taxes so that he could spend more and more money on his war. When his army was defeated by the French, John's subjects rebelled against the taxes—and against John's tyranny.

This excerpt from The Young Oxford History of Britain & Ireland *begins with John inheriting the throne of England after the death of his brother, Richard the Lionhearted.*

Richard and his wife, Berengaria of Navarre, had no children, so the next king was his brother John (1199–1216). John's claim was disputed by his young nephew, Arthur of Brittany. In 1202 John captured Arthur who disappeared and was never seen again. Everyone believed that John had ordered his murder. So when King Philip of France attacked John's French lands in Anjou and Normandy, few were willing to fight for him. As a result he quickly lost them to the king of France, and from then on he was known as "Softsword."

John spent the next ten years taxing his subjects heavily, especially his richer ones, to raise the huge sums he needed to pay for a grand military alliance against France. Unfortunately for John, the allied army was defeated at the battle of Bouvines in 1214. The English people, led by the barons, had had enough of high taxes. They rebelled and the citizens of London opened their gates to the rebels. This forced John to meet their leaders at Runnymede by the river Thames in 1215. There they forced him to make promises which were written in the treaty later known as Magna Carta.

John promised to treat everyone more fairly, and agreed to have a committee of twenty-five barons to whom people could complain if they thought he was failing to keep his promises. In fact, as everyone had suspected, John did not keep his promises. Many barons then chose Louis, the son of Philip of France, to be king of England and in May 1216 a French army held London and Winchester. When John died in 1216 the country was divided by civil war. As a king John had turned out to be a failure. He had lost Normandy and Anjou, and much of England too. Although he had many enemies, he almost never dared face them. A song-writer of the time wrote,

No man may ever trust him,

For his heart is soft and cowardly.

John's eldest son, Henry, was only nine and therefore a "minor," so a number of barons formed a council to defeat Louis and to govern until Henry III was old enough to rule for himself. The leader of the "minority council" was William Marshal, now Earl of Pembroke and a famous old warrior. William beat the French in battle. The council reissued Magna Carta to show that they intended to govern the country better than John had done. From now on Magna Carta became a symbol of good government. For the next hundred years, whenever people thought a king was being tyrannical they reminded him of Magna Carta.

Date ____________________

Name ____________________

Week 19
Day Three

Narration/Dictation Exercise

From *The Young Oxford History of Britain & Ireland* by Mike Corbishley and Kenneth O. Morgan

Date ____________________

Name ____

Week 19
Day Four

Dictation Exercise

Date ______________________

Name ______________________

Week 19
Day Five

Creative Writing

This page is left blank intentionally.

"The Garden of Live Flowers"
from *Through the Looking-Glass*
by Lewis Carroll

This passage is from the sequel to Alice in Wonderland. *Alice has gotten through the mirror in her sitting-room and has found herself in a magical land behind it. As she walks along through this land, she finds herself walking through a flower-garden.*

When you read, remember that "ough" in "bough" is pronounced like "ow" as in "now."

"O Tiger-lily," said Alice, addressing herself to one that was waving gracefully about in the wind, "I *wish* you could talk!"

"We *can* talk," said the Tiger-lily, "when there's anybody worth talking to."

Alice was so astonished that she could not speak for a minute: it quite seemed to take her breath away. At length, as the Tiger-lily only went on waving about, she spoke again, in a timid voice—almost in a whisper. "And can *all* the flowers talk?"

"As well as *you* can," said the Tiger-lily. "And a great deal louder."

"It isn't manners for us to begin, you know," said the Rose, "and I really was wondering when you'd speak! Said I to myself, 'Her face has got *some* sense in it, thought it's not a clever one!' Still, you're the right colour, and that goes a long way."

"I don't care about the colour," the Tiger-lily remarked. "If only her petals curled up a little more, she'd be all right."

Alice didn't like being criticised, so she began asking questions. "Aren't you sometimes frightened at being planted out here, with nobody to take care of you?"

"There's the tree in the middle," said the Rose. "What else is it good for?"

"But what could it do, if any danger came?" Alice asked.

"It says 'Bough-wow!' cried a Daisy. "That's why its branches are called boughs!"

"Didn't you know *that*?" cried another Daisy, and here they all began shouting together, till the air seemed quite full of little shrill voices.

"Silence, every one of you!" cried the Tiger-lily, waving itself passionately from side to side, and trembling with excitement. "They know I can't get at them!" it panted, bending its quivering head towards Alice, "or they wouldn't dare to do it!"

"Never mind!" Alice said in a soothing tone, and stooping down to the daisies, who were just beginning again, she whispered, "If you don't hold your tongues, I'll pick you!"

There was silence in a moment, and several of the pink daisies turned white.

"That's right!" said the Tiger-lily. "The daisies are worst of all. When one speaks, they all begin together, and it's enough to make one wither to hear the way they go on!"

"How is it you can all talk so nicely?" Alice said, hoping to get it into a better temper by a compliment. "I've been in many gardens before, but none of the flowers could talk."

"Put your hand down, and feel the ground," said the Tiger-lily. "Then you'll know why."

Alice did so. "It's very hard," she said, "but I don't see what that has to do with it."

"In most gardens," the Tiger-lily said, "they make the beds too soft—so that the flowers are always asleep."

This sounded a very good reason, and Alice was quite pleased to know it. "I never thought of that before!" she said.

Date ____________________

Name ____________________

Week 20
Day One

Narration Exercise

From "The Garden of Live Flowers" by Lewis Carroll

Date ______________________

Name ____

Week 20
Day Two

Dictation Exercise

"Queen Alice"
from *Through the Looking-Glass*
by Lewis Carroll

This chapter is near the end of the book. Alice has found herself in the middle of a life-size chess game and has unexpectedly been made a queen. The other two queens, the Red and White Queens, have invited her to a dinner party in her honor.

Alice glanced nervously along the table, as she walked up the large hall, and noticed that there were about fifty guests, of all kinds: some were animals, some birds, and there were even a few flowers among them. "I'm glad they've come without waiting to be asked," she thought. "I should never have known who were the right people to invite!"

There were three chairs at the head of the table; the Red and White Queens had already taken two of them, but the middle one was empty. Alice sat down in it, rather uncomfortable in the silence, and longing for some one to speak.

At last the Red Queen began. "You've missed the soup and fish," she said. "Put on the joint!" And the waiters set a leg of mutton before Alice, who looked at it rather anxiously, as she had never had to carve a joint before.

"You look a little shy; let me introduce you to that leg of mutton," said the Red Queen. "Alice—Mutton; Mutton—Alice." The leg of mutton got up in the dish and made a little bow to Alice; and Alice returned the bow, not knowing whether to be frightened or amused.

"May I give you a slice?" she said, taking up the knife and fork, and looking from one Queen to the other.

"Certainly not," the Red Queen said, very decidedly. "It isn't etiquette to cut any one you've been introduced to. Remove the joint!" And the waiters carried it off, and brought a large plum-pudding in its place.

"I won't be introduced to the pudding, please," Alice said rather hastily, "or we shall get no dinner at all. May I give you some?"

But the Red Queen looked sulky, and growled "Pudding—Alice; Alice—Pudding. Remove the pudding!" and the waiters took it away so quickly that Alice couldn't return its bow.

However, she didn't see why the Red Queen should be the only one to give orders, so, as an experiment, she called out "Waiter! Bring back the pudding!" and there it was again in a moment like a conjuring-trick. It was so large that she couldn't help feeling a LITTLE shy with it, as she had been with the mutton; however, she conquered her shyness by a great effort and cut a slice and handed it to the Red Queen.

"What impertinence!" said the Pudding. "I wonder how you'd like it, if I were to cut a slice out of YOU, you creature!"

It spoke in a thick, suety sort of voice, and Alice hadn't a word to say in reply: she could only sit and look at it and gasp.

"Make a remark," said the Red Queen: "it's ridiculous to leave all the conversation to the pudding!"

Date

Week 20
Day Three

Name

Narration/Dictation Exercise

From "Queen Alice" by Lewis Carroll

Date ____________________

Name ____

Week 20
Day Four

Dictation Exercise

Date ____________________

Week 20
Day Five

Name ____

Creative Writing

This page is left blank intentionally.

Date ________________________

Name ____

Week 21
Day One

Poetry Exercise

"Stopping by Woods on a Snowy Evening"

by Robert Frost

Whose woods these are I think I know. __________
His house is in the village though; __________
He will not see me stopping here __________
To watch his woods fill up with snow. __________
My little horse must think it queer __________
To stop without a farmhouse near __________
Between the woods and frozen lake __________
The darkest evening of the year. __________
He gives his harness bells a shake __________
To ask if there is some mistake. __________
The only other sound's the sweep __________
Of easy wind and downy flake. __________
The woods are lovely, dark and deep. __________
But I have promises to keep, __________
And miles to go before I sleep, __________
And miles to go before I sleep. __________

Whose **woods** these **are** I **think** I **know.**
His **house** is **in** the **vill**age **though**;

meter (unstress **stress**): ______________________

Date

Name

Week 21
Day Two

Dictation Exercise

Date ______________________ Week 21
Day Three

Name ____

Poetry Exercise

"The Listeners"

by Walter de la Mare

"Is there anybody there?" said the Traveller,
Knocking on the moonlit door; ____A____
And his horse in the silence champed the grasses
Of the forest's ferny floor: ____A____
And a bird flew up out of the turret,
Above the Traveller's head: ________
And he smote upon the door again a second time;
"Is there anybody there?" he said. ________
But no one descended to the Traveller;
No head from the leaf-fringed sill ________
Leaned over and looked into his grey eyes,
Where he stood perplexed and still. ________
But only a host of phantom listeners
That dwelt in the lone house then ________
Stood listening in the quiet of the moonlight
To that voice from the world of men: ________
Stood thronging the faint moonbeams on the dark stair,
That goes down to the empty hall, ________
Hearkening in an air stirred and shaken
By the lonely Traveller's call. ________
And he felt in his heart their strangeness,
Their stillness answering his cry, ________
While his horse moved, cropping the dark turf,
'Neath the starred and leafy sky; ________
For he suddenly smote on the door, even
Louder, and lifted his head:— ________
"Tell them I came, and no one answered,
That I kept my word," he said. ________
Never the least stir made the listeners,
Though every word he spake ________
Fell echoing through the shadowiness of the still house
From the one man left awake: ________
Ay, they heard his foot upon the stirrup,
And the sound of iron on stone, ________
And how the silence surged softly backward,
When the plunging hoofs were gone. ________

Week 21
Day Three

"Is there anybody there?" said the **Traveller**,
Knocking on the moonlit door; A
And his horse in the silence champed the **grasses**
Of the forest's ferny floor: A
And a bird flew up out of the **turret,**
Above the Traveller's head: B
And he smote upon the door again a second **time**;
"Is there anybody there?" he said. B
But no one descended to the **Traveller**;
No head from the leaf-fringed sill C
Leaned over and looked into his grey **eyes**,
Where he stood perplexed and still. C
But only a host of phantom **listeners**
That dwelt in the lone house then D
Stood listening in the quiet of the **moonlight**
To that voice from the world of men: D
Stood thronging the faint moonbeams on the dark **stair**,
That goes down to the empty hall, E
Hearkening in an air stirred and **shaken**
By the lonely Traveller's call. E
And he felt in his heart their **strangeness**,
Their stillness answering his cry, F
While his horse moved, cropping the dark **turf**,
'Neath the starred and leafy sky; F
For he suddenly smote on the door, **even**
Louder, and lifted his head:— B
"Tell them I came, and no one **answered**,
That I kept my word," he said. B
Never the least stir made the **listeners**,
Though every word he spake G
Fell echoing through the shadowiness of the still **house**
From the one man left awake: G
Ay, they heard his foot upon the **stirrup**,
And the sound of iron on stone, H
And how the silence surged softly **backward**,
When the plunging hoofs were gone. H

Knocking **on** the **moon**lit **door**;

stress unstress **stress** unstress **stress** unstress **stress**

And his **horse** in the **si**lence **champed** the **grass**es

unstress unstress **stress** unstress unstress **stress** unstress **stress** unstress **stress** unstress

And a **bird** flew **up** out **of** the **tur**ret,

unstress unstress **stress** unstress **stress** unstress **stress** unstress **stress** unstress

But **no** one de**scen**ded **to** the **Trav**eller;

unstress **stress** unstress unstress **stress** unstress **stress** unstress **stress** unstress

Their **still**ness **an**swering his **cry**,

unstress **stress** unstress **stress** unstress unstress unstress **stress**

Never the **least stir** made the **list**eners,

stress unstress unstress **stress stress** unstress unstress **stress** unstress unstress

And the **sound** of **ir**on on **stone**,

unstress unstress **stress** unstress **stress** unstress unstress **stress**

Date ____________________

Name ____

Dictation Exercise

Date ____________________

Name ____________________

Week 21
Day Five

Creative Writing

This page is left blank intentionally.

From *The Furious Flycycle*

by Jan Wahl

The hero of this book, Melvin Spitznagle, is going to invent a contraption that will make his bicycle do something unusual. Can you guess what it is? (Hint: look at the title of the book.)

"Orphan Asylum" is an old name for an orphanage, a place where children without parents lived.

The house in town that had the most shutters, a spooky turret, a cat named Tweet about to have babies, an ancient spreading apple tree with lots of red apples, and a barn in back with spires sticking up and fancy woodcarving, was the house on Bean Road in which lived Melvin Spitznagle.

Melvin was considered lucky; his father owned the Ice Cream Works on Radish Street, where they wholesaled and manufactured Spitznagle's Ice Cream. There was a freezer with a capacity of six tons a day; and the business included a fifteen horsepower engine. The annual output was between twenty thousand and thirty thousand gallons. It was the most important ice cream works in the County. Melvin liked to walk past the big plant and read the sign, with letters in faded gold and blue, that said:

SPITZNAGLE'S ICE CREAM
"Better than it sounds"

Because his father was the ice cream maker, Melvin grew pretty popular at school. His father brought home, in five-gallon containers, the ice cream not sold to stores within a week. So Melvin's schoolmates trooped hungrily off to Bean Road after school, and they would sit on the white-painted benches and lawn chairs in the Spitznagle back yard politely but eagerly, wondering which flavor Emma Dudd, the maid, was going to bring out. It was vanilla most often.

But with jams and sauces and different syrups (which they brought with them) added, Melvin's schoolmates could vary the flavors as they chose. Emma Dudd was kept busy zipping back and forth from the kitchen, and usually her linen maid's cap fell over her eyes as she hurried.

Thus Melvin never lacked for company. However, in his heart, he wished he were enjoyed for himself alone; with the result that suddenly one day he asked his father to give the unsold ice cream, in its five-gallon containers, to the county Orphan Asylum instead. Nobody much came to the back yard after that, except two fat little girls, the Sprenger sisters, Mavis and Edna—who wanted to play croquet.

Melvin said "Pooh Pooh!" to everybody and decided to spend his time becoming a scientific mechanical wizard.

He was handy at repairing bicycles. And people soon began showing up with broken chains and sprung sockets for him to fix. Again, however, Melvin began to feel he was not being appreciated for what he was himself.

So he pleaded with his parents and got them to let him use the unused barn for his private workshop.

He outfitted the place with wonderful tools—handdrills, wrenches, pronged and prongless hammers, pliers, vises, screwdrivers, files, saws, chisels, soldering irons, and other things.

On the door he put a sign:

BEWARE!! GROUCHY PERSON

Date ______________________________

Name ______________________________

Week 22
Day One

Narration Exercise

From *The Furious Flycycle* by Jan Wahl

Date

Name

Week 22
Day Two

Dictation Exercise

From *The Furious Flycycle*

by Jan Wahl

This is the next part of The Furious Flycycle. *It tells what happens after Melvin establishes his mechanical workshop.*

When Emma Dudd was missing the eggbeater, she knew where it had gone. When Melvin's mother's sewing machine was missing some of its parts, she knew where they had disappeared to.

Yet always, when Melvin returned a thing (which he did, having learned its secret), it was better than new; he *was* a mechanical wizard. The eggbeater then became the fastest in town, the sewing machine stitched quicker and better than before.

One hot July day the freezer at his father's plant broke down. The ice cream came flooding out into a huge mound onto Radish Street.

The town fire department arrived, starting to work with shovels. Soon, all the dogs and cats in town heard about it and were there, licking up the rainbow-colored treat—the cherry, peach, lime, vanilla, strawberry, chocolate!

Melvin raced across town with his tool kit. He went straight to the source of the trouble—a loose rotary four-gauge Whirlogax—pulled out his #7 roman wrench, and, in a jiffy, had everything under control. The fire department stood there amazed. Mr. Spitznagle did not have to send his employees home.

A few days later a truck pulled up on Bean Road.

The expressman wheeled up to the door a dazzling object—a new Silver Zephyr bicycle. Attached to it was a tag reading IN GRATITUDE. YOUR FATHER.

Melvin took a few days off from his workshop to pedal the Silver Zephyr up and down the streets. He even went outside of town, trying country roads. There the riding got bumpy. Melvin wished he were able to ride as fast as a tornado. He drove everywhere with a dreamy look in his eyes, narrowly missing flocks of chickens and yipping dogs; Melvin was lost in thought.

Then Fate stepped into his life. Fate was an old, old man in battered top hat and shaggy beard.

Professor Mickimecki, with beard, top hat, with a red-bulb nose, with his hose torn, wearing worn carpet slippers in place of shoes, the great inventor Professor Mickimecki (formerly of Prague, Stuttgart, Liverpool, and Bombay) had shot through town on the Rapid Pearl Express, which came through once a week without stopping on its way to points West.

As the train raced through, Professor Mickimecki had pulled the emergency cord. "STOP THE TRAIN!" he shouted, tossing his valises out the window to the surprise of fellow passengers.

Then he scrambled out himself, holding onto his top hat.

"This is the town in which I want to spend the rest of my life. *Unnoticed!"*

That very same afternoon the Professor rented, with one hundred dollars down in two-dollar bills, the old Ketcham house.

Soon he painted the house green, so that it looked like grass. The fleet of trucks that came bringing his many large crates and boxes had a hard time finding it.

It was an inspiration to Melvin just to know so great a man lived now in town.

Date ______________________

Week 22
Day Three

Name ______________________________________

Narration/Dictation Exercise

From *The Furious Flycycle* by Jan Wahl

Date ______________________

Name ______________________________________

Week 22
Day Four

Dictation Exercise

Date ______________________

Name ____

Creative Writing

This page is left blank intentionally.

"Two Great Painters" from *Fifty Famous People: A Book of Short Stories*

by James Baldwin

A long time ago in Ancient Greece, there were no cameras or photographs. If people wanted a picture of something, they had to paint it by hand. This story is about two famous painters who had a contest to see who could make the most lifelike picture. These two artists really did live over 2,000 years ago. But the story of their contest wasn't written down until many years later (by a Roman named Pliny the Elder). So, we don't know for sure if it really happened—but it's a great story that people have enjoyed telling for a long, long time.

There was once a painter whose name was Zeuxis (ZOOK-suhs). He could paint pictures so life-like that they were mistaken for the real things which they represented.

One day, he painted a picture of some fruit which looked so real that the birds flew down and pecked at it. This made him very proud of his skill.

"I am the only man in the world who can paint a picture so true to life," he said.

There was another famous artist whose name was Parrhasius (puh-RAY-see-us).

When he heard of the boast which Zeuxis had made, he said to himself, "I will see what I can do." So he painted a beautiful picture which seemed to be covered with a curtain. Then he invited Zeuxis to come and see it.

Zeuxis looked at it closely. "Draw the curtain aside and show us the picture," he said. Parrhasius laughed and answered, "The curtain is the picture."

"Well," said Zeuxis, "you have beaten me this time, and I shall boast no more. I deceived only the birds, but you have deceived me, a painter."

Some time after this, Zeuxis painted another wonderful picture. It was that of a boy carrying a basket of ripe red cherries. When he hung this painting outside his door, some birds flew down and tried to carry the cherries away.

"Ah! This picture is a failure," he said. "For if the boy had been as well painted as the cherries, the birds would have been afraid to come near him."

Date ______________________

Name ____

Week 23
Day One

Narration Exercise

"Two Great Painters" from *Fifty Famous People: A Book of Short Stories*

by James Baldwin

Date

Name

Week 23
Day Two

Dictation Exercise

This page is left blank intentionally.

"Samuel Finley Breese Morse" from *The Child's Book of American Biography*

by Mary Stoyell Stimpson

Long before the telephone was invented, people had no quick way to send messages across long distances. Samuel Morse had a clever idea. He invented a special code made of dots and dashes that could travel through a wire! He called his invention the telegraph. But when Samuel first started telling people about it, many didn't believe it would work.

Morse expected others to be as pleased as he with his invention, but they did not even believe in it. "The idea," they said, "that a man in New York can talk with another in San Francisco!"

Of course, if people did not believe Morse's idea was right, they naturally would not give any money to try it out, so for years this man almost starved while he lived in one small room that had to serve for work-shop, bedroom, kitchen, and studio, while he took pupils, did small pictures, anything, in fact, to get money for his machine and to pay for his room and food.

You see he needed one beautifully made machine, and he must have a long line of poles and wires built before he could prove that with his dots and dashes people could talk to each other, although they were miles apart. And this would cost a lot of money.

He sent many letters to Congress asking for help. The men in Congress were not interested. His letters were not answered. "Poor old chap," they laughed, "he's gone crazy over his scheme!"

Finally, as no attention was paid to his letters, Mr. Morse saved up a little money and went to Washington himself. One senator agreed to ask the Congress to advance him some money. But the time kept slipping by, and nothing was done.

One night when it was late, and all the senators were eager to get through with bills and business, the senator who liked Mr. Morse saw him sitting away up in the gallery, all alone. He went up to him and said: "I know your bill (or request) will not pass. Oh, give it up and go home!"

When Mr. Morse went out of the building, he had given up all hopes of getting help. He went to his boarding-house, and when he had paid for the room and his breakfast the next morning, he had just thirty-seven cents left in the world.

But the next morning—what do you think?—a young lady, the daughter of a government official who supported the telegraph idea, came rushing into the room where Mr. Morse was eating his breakfast, and holding out both hands, said joyfully: "I've come to congratulate you. Your bill has passed!"

"It cannot be," he answered.

"Oh, it is true. My father let me be the bearer of the good news."

"Well," said Mr. Morse, trembling with delight, "you, my dear message-bearer, shall send the first message that ever goes across the wires."

It did not take long to convince the world that Professor Morse (as he was now called) had invented a fine thing. In less than a year a line was completed from Washington to Baltimore, and Miss Ellsworth, the government official's daughter, sent the first message ever heard over a recording telegraph.

Name ______________________ Date ______________________

Narration/Dictation Exercise

"Samuel Finley Breese Morse" from *The Child's Book of American Biography* by Mary Stoyell Stimpson

Date ____________________

Name ____________________

Week 23
Day Four

Dictation Exercise

Date ____________________

Name ____

Week 23
Day Five

Creative Writing

This page is left blank intentionally.

From *Mrs. Piggle-Wiggle's Magic*
by Betty MacDonald

Mrs. Piggle-Wiggle is a little woman who can cure any bad habit that children have. In this story, she has to cure a brother and sister who are tattletales! The first excerpt describes just how bad the problem is. Wendy, who is nine, and Timmy, who is seven, have just come home from school—and their mother, Mrs. Hamilton, is about to find out just how bad the two children really are.

"And how was school?" she asked Wendy as she helped her off with her coat and leggings.

Wendy said, "Well, I hate everybody at school and everybody at school hates me."

Mrs. Hamilton was shocked. Wendy was nine years old. She had nice fat pigtails, shiny brown bangs, sparkling brown eyes and pink cheeks. Mrs. Hamilton didn't see how anyone could hate her. She said, "Why Wendy, that's dreadful, dear. Why does everyone hate you?"

Wendy said, "I don't know. They just do. And I don't care because I hate everybody." She sat down at the kitchen table and took a bite of sugar cookie.

Timmy, who was seven, was sitting on the floor taking off his leggings. His mother said, "Here, Timmy, let me help you."

Timmy said, "No thanks. I can do it myself. You want to know why everybody hates Wendy—it's because she's such an old tattletale. She tells the teacher on everybody. I hate her too."

Mrs. Hamilton said, "Why, Wendy Hamilton. Do you tell on people?"

Wendy said with evident pride, "Uh, huh. I tell Miss Worthington every time anybody whispers or cheats or writes notes. I even told her when Jimmy Murton sucked his paintbrush today. We're not supposed to suck our paintbrushes; we're supposed to use our fingers to make points." She took a little sip of her cocoa and wiped her lips daintily. Wendy was very pleased with herself.

Mrs. Hamilton wasn't pleased with her. She said, "Wendy Hamilton, I think that's horrid. Telling the teacher about a little thing like sucking a paintbrush."

Timmy said, "Oh, she's always in there tattling. She's so busy spying and tattling she doesn't even have time to play."

Wendy said, "You better be careful, Mr. Timothy Hamilton, or I'll tell Mother that you haven't brushed your teeth for five nights and you gave your liver to Spot last Wednesday and you spent some of your Sunday School money on candy and last night you read in bed with a flashlight."

Timmy said, "Yeah, and this morning you put the rest of your toast in the silverware drawer, you spilled Spot's water and didn't wipe it up and you ate half the candy I bought with my Sunday School money."

Wendy, quite red in the face, said, "Oh, bah, bah, bah, to you, you old crumpet."

"Bah, bah, bah, yourself, old Dog Eyes," Timmy said.

Wendy said, "Motherrrrrrrrr, he calls me dog eyes all the time. He says only dogs have brown eyes."

Mrs. Hamilton said, "Wendy, change your school clothes and then go in and start your practicing. Timmy, change your school clothes and then go down in the basement and put away all of Daddy's tools that you got out last night. I must say, you're both so disagreeable I'm sorry you came home from school and spoiled my nice peaceful afternoon."

Date ______________________

Name ____

Week 24
Day One

Narration Exercise

From *Mrs. Piggle-Wiggle's Magic* by Betty MacDonald

Date ______________________

Name ____

Week 24
Day Two

Dictation Exercise

From *Mrs. Piggle-Wiggle's Magic*
by Betty MacDonald

Mrs. Hamilton gives Timmy and Wendy magic tattletale pills that Mrs. Piggle-Wiggle sends her. This tells what happens next! "Galoshes" is another name for rubber boots.

As Mrs. Hamilton took up her children's oatmeal and poured their milk, she glanced fearfully toward the back stairs. How would they look this time and what had the magic pills done to them? In no time at all she had her answer. First she heard shrill fighting voices, quick chasing footsteps, slaps and yelps and then racing down the stairs came the tattlers, each redfaced and anxious to tell first.

"Motherrrrrrr," said Wendy as she slid through the kitchen door. "Motherrrrrr, Timmy—" but instead of the long tattletale she intended, out of Wendy's mouth came a big puff of black smoke. The puff of smoke was shaped like a little black cloud except that hanging from the bottom of it were four little black tails. Little black tattletales. The black cloud rose to the ceiling and stuck—the four little tails swayed gently back and forth.

Timmy said, "My gosh, did you see that. Smoke came out of Wendy's mouth. Say, Mother, I bet ole Wendy's been—" but instead of saying "smoking" as he intended, a big puff of black smoke came out of his mouth. It too was a little black cloud but it had only one tail hanging from it because he had only intended to tattle about one thing. Timmy and Wendy stood with their mouths open staring at the ceiling.

Mrs. Hamilton said, "Well, I've always wondered what a tattletale looks like, now I know. Ugh, what ugly things!" Wendy and Timmy didn't say anything. They looked at the ceiling, then at each other and then back at the ceiling. Finally they sat down to breakfast.

After breakfast it was still snowing hard but Wendy and Timmy said they were going out to shovel the walks. They put on their leggings, coats, caps and mittens without a word but they couldn't decide whose galoshes were whose and they began jerking them back and forth and pushing and shoving and finally were just going to yell for Mrs. Hamilton to tattle when out of their open mouths came two huge rolls of black smoke each with a long black tattletale suspended from it. The two new tattletales soared slowly upwards and stuck to the ceiling not far from the first two.

Wendy said, "What if that happened in school?"

Timmy said, "Boy, the kids would sure be surprised. I can just hear ole Miss Harkness. She'd say, 'Timmy Hamilton, you have been SMOKING!'"

Wendy said, "I don't think I'd like to have that happen in school. All the children would laugh at me. Hey, these are your galoshes. I can tell because they are a teensy bit littler than mine."

They put on their galoshes and went quietly out to shovel the walks.

Date ____________________

Name ____________________

Week 24
Day Three

Narration/Dictation Exercise

From *Mrs. Piggle-Wiggle's Magic* by Betty MacDonald

Date ______________________

Name ______________________

Week 24
Day Four

Dictation Exercise

Date ____________________

Week 24
Day Five

Name ____________________

Creative Writing

This page is left blank intentionally.

From *Money, Money, Money: Where It Comes From, How to Save It, Spend It and Make It*

by Eve Drobot

This excerpt from Money, Money, Money *will tell you more about the names we use for money.*

The word "money" comes from Latin, the language of the ancient Romans. Juno, one of their goddesses, was nicknamed Moneta, which means "the woman who warns." Juno was called that because one of her jobs was to warn people when they were doing wrong. She was an important goddess, and her temple was an important place. So it's not surprising that the ancient Romans made their coins right next to her temple. The coins themselves soon came to be called by the goddess's nickname.

Moneta is the word modern Italians still use to describe their coins. The Spanish call theirs *moneda* and the French say *monnaie.* The place where coins are made is called a "mint."

The first coins weren't all round—some were shaped like pie wedges. The Latin word for wedge, *cuneus*, gives us the English word "coin"....

The dollar is known from Australia to Zimbabwe, in 23 countries in all. The word "dollar" originally comes from the German word *thaler*. When a German emperor became the king of Spain in the 17th century, Spanish explorers and conquerors took the German word to the Americas, and from there it kept going until it reached all around the world.

No one is absolutely sure where the $ sign came from, but there are lots of interesting theories. One of the most accepted ones is that it is the initials U and S, for United States, stuck one on top of the other—people writing the symbol in a hurry just stopped using the bottom part of the U. Another idea is that it is a mangled form of the number 8, because the Spanish coins known as "pieces of eight" were the most common coins in North America 200 years ago.

We get the word "cash" from the ancient Chinese, who carried their coins in bundles on string. A bundle of a hundred coins was called one *cash*. But the Chinese didn't invent the word, either—they got it from the Portuguese, with whom they traded, and who called their coins *caixa* (pronounced "cash-a").

In every language there are slang terms for money—or the lack of it. If you had a dollar for every nickname money has, you'd be rich. Dollars are sometimes called "bucks," for the days when North American Native peoples used buckskins, or deerhides, for trade. A hundred years ago, you'd have heard North American money being called “saddle blankets” because the bank notes were very large—large enough, people joked, to cover a horse’s back. In Latin America, money is nicknamed “little paper.” In France, money is “the ticket” or “the round stuff.” In Germany it’s known as “pinke-pinke,” for the sound coins make as they jingle in your pocket.

Date ______________________

Name ____

Week 25
Day One

Narration Exercise

From *Money, Money, Money* by Eve Drobot

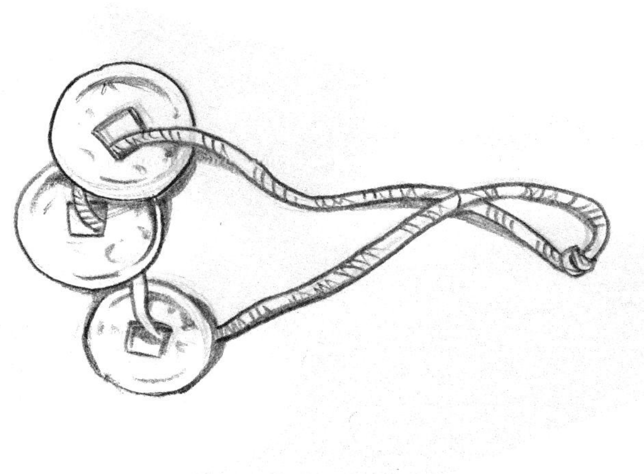

Date ______________________

Name ____

Week 25
Day Two

Dictation Exercise

From *The Everything Kids' Money Book*

by Diane Mayr

Back in the days of Benjamin Franklin and Thomas Jefferson, the colonies did not have just one kind of money. Each colony had its own kind of coin and its own mint. Listen to what happened then. To "counterfeit" means to make a false coin.

In the early days of coins, with gold and silver being such soft metals, a dishonest person was able to shave off small pieces of the edge of a coin. This was called "clipping." After a while the dishonest person would have a collection of clipped pieces large enough to be melted down and sold....

In 1651, John Hull of the Massachusetts Bay Colony started a mint that produced very crude coins. The coins were stamped with NE for New England on one side and the denomination on the other. The simplicity of the coin led to trouble—it was easy to counterfeit and easy to clip. An improved design was necessary. From 1653 to 1674, Hull's mint produced redesigned coins that had a willow, oak, or pine tree on the obverse [the front of a coin] and the date...on the reverse [the back of the coin]. Hull's coins are usually referred to as "New England pine tree" coins.

There were different coins in each of the colonies. The values placed on the coins in each region also differed and often led to confusion....Imagine how confusing things got by the end of the eighteenth century when the British had been defeated and each of the states was minting its own coins! Take for example, Connecticut. During the years 1785 to 1788, more than three hundred different copper coins were made! Why so many? The state authorized private citizens to mint the coins for the state. Each mint developed its own design!

Individual states did not always find it easy to mint their own coins. In 1787 and 1788, when the state of Massachusetts began to make copper cents and half cents, it found that it cost two cents to make each cent, and one cent to make a half cent! Massachusetts only operated its mint for a short time.

By 1787 it was time for the United States to think about producing a national coin. James Jarvis was given a contract by Congress to produce three hundred tons of copper coins. Jarvis minted a coin known as the "Fugio" cent. The Fugio cent is the first official coin of the United States.

The cent had a sundial on the obverse and the Latin word *fugio* meaning "I fly," referring to the old saying, "time flies." Also on the obverse is the legend [saying] "mind your business." Mind your business refers to the citizens of the United States having to build up their businesses to make for a stronger country. It had nothing to do with nosiness!

The reverse of the Fugio cent had a chain with thirteen links representing the thirteen states, and the motto "We are one."

Date ____________________

Name ____

Week 25
Day Three

Narration/Dictation Exercise

From *The Everything Kids' Money Book* by Diane Mayr

Date ______________________

Name ____

Dictation Exercise

Date ______________________

Name ____

Creative Writing

From *Babe: The Gallant Pig*

by Dick King-Smith

Babe *tells the story of a very unusual pig. When he is a little piglet, he is won at a fair by Farmer Hogget, who brings him back to the Hogget farm. There, the collie Fly and her four puppies meet the piglet for the first time. The puppies have never seen a pig before; they ask their mother if pigs are stupid, and Fly tells them yes.*

A "loose box" is a barn stall, used for horses or other livestock.

The floor of the stables had not rung to a horse's hoof for many years, but it was a useful place for storing things. The hens foraged about there, and sometimes laid their eggs in the old wooden mangers; the swallows built their nests against its roof beams with mud from the duck pond; and rats and mice lived happy lives in its shelter until the farm cats cut them short. At one end of the stables were two loose boxes with boarded sides topped by iron rails. One served as a kennel for Fly and her puppies. The other sometimes housed sick sheep. In there Farmer Hogget had put the piglet.

A convenient stack of straw bales allowed the dogs to look down into the box through the bars.

"It certainly looks stupid," said one of the puppies, yawning. At the sound of the words the piglet glanced up quickly. He put his head to one side and regarded the dogs with sharp eyes. Something about the sight of this very small animal standing all by itself in the middle of the roomy loose box touched Fly's soft heart. Already she was sorry that she had said that pigs were stupid, for this one certainly did not appear to be so. Also there was something dignified about the way it stood its ground, in a strange place, confronted with strange animals. How different from the silly sheep, who at the mere sight of a dog would run aimlessly about, crying "Wolf! Wolf!" in their empty-headed way.

"Hullo," she said. "Who are you?"

"I'm a Large White," said the piglet.

"Blimey!" said one of the puppies. "If that's a large white, what's a small one like?" And they all four sniggered.

"Be quiet!" snapped Fly. "Just remember that five minutes ago you didn't even know what a pig was." And to the piglet she said kindly, "I expect that's your breed, dear. I meant, what's your name?"

"I don't know," said the piglet.

"Well, what did your mother call you, to tell you apart from your brothers and sisters?" said Fly and then wished she hadn't, for at the mention of his family the piglet began to look distinctly unhappy. His little forehead wrinkled and he gulped and his voice trembled as he answered.

"She called us all the same."

"And what was that, dear?"

"Babe," said the piglet, and the puppies began to giggle until their mother silenced them with a growl.

"But that's a lovely name," she said. "Would you like us to call you that? It'll make you feel more at home."

At this last word the little pig's face fell even further.

"I want my mum," he said very quietly.

At that instant the collie made up her mind that she would foster this unhappy child.

"Go out in the yard and play," she said to the puppies, and she climbed to the top of the straw stack and jumped over the rail and down into the loose box beside the piglet.

"Listen, Babe," she said. "You've got to be a brave boy. Everyone has to leave their mother, it's all part of growing up. I did it, when I was your age, and my puppies will have to leave me quite soon. But I'll look after you. If you like." Then she licked his little snout with a warm rough tongue, her plumed tail wagging.

"There. Is that nice?" she said.

Date ____________________

Name ____

Week 26
Day One

Narration Exercise

From *Babe: The Gallant Pig* by Dick King-Smith

Date

Name

Week 26
Day Two

Dictation Exercise

From *Babe: The Gallant Pig*

by Dick King-Smith

Fly's puppies grow up to be sheepdogs, and Babe asks his new mother why he can't be a sheep-pig. Fly agrees to teach Babe how to herd ducks—but she doesn't think that her foster child will ever be able to herd sheep properly. In this next part of the story, Babe meets a real sheep for the first time.

"Ewe" is the proper name for a female sheep. It is pronounced just like "you."

Farmer Hogget and Fly had been out around the flock, and when they returned Fly was driving before her an old lame ewe, which they penned in the loose box where the piglet had originally been shut. Then they went away up the hill again.

Babe made his way into the stables, curious to meet this, the first of the animals that he planned one day to work with, but he could not see into the box. He snuffled under the bottom of the door, and from inside there came a cough and the sharp stamp of a foot, and then the sound of a hoarse complaining voice.

"Wolves! Wolves!" it said. "They never do leave a body alone. Nag, nag, nag all day long, go here, go there, do this, do that. What d'you want now? Can't you give us a bit of peace, wolf?"

"I'm not a wolf," said Babe under the door.

"Oh, I knows all that," said the sheep sourly. "Calls yourself a sheepdog, I knows that, but you don't fool none of us. You're a wolf like the rest of 'em, given half a chance. You looks at us, and you sees lamb chops. Go away, wolf."

"But I'm not a sheepdog either," said Babe, and he scrambled up the stack of straw bales and looked over the bars.

"You see?" he said.

"Well I'll be dipped," said the old sheep peering up at him. "No more you ain't. What are you?"

"Pig," said Babe. "Large White. What are you?"

"Ewe," said the sheep.

"No, not me, you—what are you?"

"I'm a ewe."

Mum was right, thought Babe, they certainly are stupid. But if I'm going to learn how to be a sheep-pig I must try to understand them, and this might be a good chance. Perhaps I could make a friend of this one.

"My name's Babe," he said in a jolly voice. "What's yours?"

"Maaaaa," said the sheep.

"That's a nice name," said Babe. "What's the matter with you, Ma?"

"Foot rot," said the sheep, holding up a foreleg. "And I've got a nasty cough." She coughed. "And I'm not as young as I was."

"You don't look very old to me," said Babe politely.

A look of pleasure came over the sheep's mournful face, and she lay down in the straw.

"Very civil of you to say so," she said. "First kind word I've had since I were a little lamb," and she belched loudly and began to chew a mouthful of cud.

Date ______________________

Week 26
Day Three

Name ______________________________________

Narration/Dictation Exercise

From *Babe: The Gallant Pig* by Dick King-Smith

Date ______________________________

Name ____

Week 26
Day Four

Dictation Exercise

Date ____________________________

Name ____

Week 26
Day Five

Creative Writing

I woke up because something was scratching me. I was lying in a bed of straw. "Where am I? Where is my bed?" I wondered. Then I saw my reflection in a pane of glass lying in the barn . . . "I am a pig!" . . .

This page is left blank intentionally.

From *Hunting and Herding Dogs*

by Marie-Therese Miller

Fly and Babe are characters in a story, but farmers really do use collies (although not pigs!) to herd sheep. This selection describes how shepherds work with their dogs.

The handler and his black-and-white border collie enter the field. A flock of sheep stands grazing in the pasture. The handler holds a shepherd's crook, a long staff with a curve at the top, in his hand. He has a whistle tied around his neck. The handler whistles a command: "Away to me." The dog responds by running counterclockwise around the sheep. What happens next is a telltale sign that border collies are born to herd.

When the dog is behind the sheep, the handler tells it to lie down. The border collie stops in a crouch, with its shoulders down and its rear end up. The dog glares at the sheep. This stare is called "eye," and it helps convince the sheep to move away from the dog. "Walk up," the handler orders, and the dog slowly approaches the sheep. The sheep gather, as if following the dog's strict orders. The border collie collects the herd and walks the sheep directly to the handler.

The border collie has a natural instinct to gather stock and bring it toward the handler. With training that builds on this natural ability, the border collie can be an invaluable tool to sheep farmers.

Border collies are superb herding dogs that are known for their intelligence. By the time they are trained to herd, border collies understand nearly 20 different commands. Border collies also have the ability to work independently. On big farms, the dogs often herd out of sight of their handlers and must solve problems on their own.

This dog breed has lots of energy and loves to herd. The dog's shoulder-down stance and staring "eye" make it seem like a predator to the sheep. When a dog approaches the sheep herd like this, the group instinctively moves away. This is another reason border collies are successful at herding work....

In more advanced training, a border collie learns to move, or drive, the sheep herd away from the handler. Driving is difficult to teach a border collie because it goes against the breed's gathering instinct, to move the sheep toward the farmer. Driving is easier for the dog to learn if the sheep are placed in a narrow lane with fences on either side and with the handler and the dog behind the herd. This way, the dog cannot race around the sheep and gather them back to the handler. Soon, the dog will grasp the driving concept and the enclosed area will no longer be needed.

Date ________________________

Name ____

Week 27
Day One

Narration Exercise

From *Hunting and Herding Dogs* by Marie-Therese Miller

Date ____________________

Name ____

Week 27
Day Two

Dictation Exercise

This page is left blank intentionally.

From *A Dog's World*

edited by Christine Hunsicker

An American woman named Susan Allen Toth wrote this description of an English sheepdog trial. It is found in a book called A Dog's World, *which is a collection of essays and stories written by many different people. A woman named Christine Hunsicker had the job of putting all the essays and stories together into one book. We call her the book's "editor," and instead of saying that the book is "by Christine Hunsicker" (since so many other people wrote parts of it!), we say that the book is "edited by Christine Hunsicker."*

When a sheepdog leaves the post, he begins his *outrun,* the first phase of the trial. To avoid coming at the sheep head-on, and alarming or scattering them, the dog circles widely to the right or left....When the dog contacts the sheep, he has completed his second phase, the *lift.* Now he must drive the little flock back toward his handler.

Watching the eager border collies streak up the field, James and I could scarcely believe their speed. Crouching low, a black-and-white blur in the tall grass, a dog usually reached the end of the field in moments. "Oh yes," our neighbor assured us, "he can get up to forty miles an hour, can a good dog."

Speed is not the only consideration, however. In the third phase, the *fetch,* as the dog brings the sheep down the field, he is supposed to herd them in a straight line. But sheep do not like straight lines. They have their own ideas.

Nor do they have any desire to cooperate in the *drive,* the next phase, a triangular course that passes through two-gate obstacles. The dog is supposed to move, turn, and keep the sheep in line without upsetting them....Sheep have the irritating habit of bolting this way or that, separating from the flock without warning, or turning at the last possible moment to skirt a gate....

In the final two phases of the trial, the *shed* and *pen,* the dog has to perform even more intricate maneuvers. First, at a signal, the dog must identify two sheep specially marked by large collars and then cut them off from the flock. Finally, after again collecting the sheep, the dog is supposed to herd them into a pen. The sheep do not tend to file into the pen without a fuss. The handler, standing at the gate of the pen and holding it open, can wave his shepherd's staff and try to block the meandering sheep with his body, but he or she cannot let go of the gate.

Date ____________________

Name ____________________

Narration/Dictation Exercise

From *A Dog's World* edited by Christine Hunsicker

Outrun: leaving the post
Lift: making contact with the sheep
Fetch: bringing the sheep to the handler
Drive: herding the sheep through gates
Shed: cutting two particular sheep off from the rest of the flock
Pen: herding all of the sheep into a pen

Date ______________________

Week 27
Day Four

Name ______________________________________

Dictation Exercise

Date ____________________

Name ____

Creative Writing

From *Anne of Green Gables*

by Lucy Maud Montgomery

Marilla and Matthew Cuthbert are an elderly brother and sister who live together on Prince Edward Island, in Canada. They decide that they need help on their farm, so they send away to an orphanage in a nearby town, asking for a boy who can come live with them. Matthew Cuthbert goes to pick up the orphan at the train station—but when he gets there, he finds that they've sent a little girl instead. He doesn't know what to do, so he takes the little girl home.

Marilla came briskly forward as Matthew opened the door. But when her eyes fell on the odd little figure in the stiff, ugly dress, with the long braids of red hair and the eager, luminous eyes, she stopped short in amazement.

"Matthew Cuthbert, who's that?" she ejaculated. "Where is the boy?"

"There wasn't any boy," said Matthew wretchedly. "There was only HER."

He nodded at the child, remembering that he had never even asked her name.

"No boy! But there MUST have been a boy," insisted Marilla. "We sent word to Mrs. Spencer to bring a boy."

"Well, she didn't. She brought HER. I asked the station-master. And I had to bring her home. She couldn't be left there, no matter where the mistake had come in."

"Well, this is a pretty piece of business!" ejaculated Marilla.

During this dialogue the child had remained silent, her eyes roving from one to the other, all the animation fading out of her face. Suddenly she seemed to grasp the full meaning of what had been said. Dropping her precious carpet-bag she sprang forward a step and clasped her hands.

"You don't want me!" she cried. "You don't want me because I'm not a boy! I might have expected it. Nobody ever did want me. I might have known it was all too beautiful to last. I might have known nobody really did want me. Oh, what shall I do? I'm going to burst into tears!"

Burst into tears she did. Sitting down on a chair by the table, flinging her arms out upon it, and burying her face in them, she proceeded to cry stormily. Marilla and Matthew looked at each other deprecatingly across the stove. Neither of them knew what to say or do. Finally Marilla stepped lamely into the breach.

"Well, well, there's no need to cry so about it."

"Yes, there IS need!" The child raised her head quickly, revealing a tear-stained face and trembling lips. "YOU would cry, too, if you were an orphan and had come to a place you thought was going to be home and found that they didn't want you because you weren't a boy. Oh, this is the most TRAGICAL thing that ever happened to me!"

Something like a reluctant smile, rather rusty from long disuse, mellowed Marilla's grim expression.

"Well, don't cry any more. We're not going to turn you out-of-doors to-night. You'll have to stay here until we investigate this affair. What's your name?"

The child hesitated for a moment.

"Will you please call me Cordelia?" she said eagerly.

"CALL you Cordelia? Is that your name?"

"No-o-o, it's not exactly my name, but I would love to be called Cordelia. It's such a perfectly elegant name."

"I don't know what on earth you mean. If Cordelia isn't your name, what is?"

"Anne Shirley," reluctantly faltered forth the owner of that name, "but, oh, please do call me Cordelia. It can't matter much to you what you call me if I'm only going to be here a little while, can it? And Anne is such an unromantic name."

"Unromantic fiddlesticks!" said the unsympathetic Marilla. "Anne is a real good plain sensible name. You've no need to be ashamed of it."

Date ______________________

Name ____

Week 28
Day One

Narration Exercise

From *Anne of Green Gables* by Lucy Maud Montgomery

Date ____________________

Name ____

Week 28
Day Two

Dictation Exercise

From *Pioneers in Canada*

by Harry Johnston

Pioneers in Canada is *a classic text about Canadian history written by Harry Johnston almost a hundred years ago. Johnston describes the journey that the French explorer Jacques Cartier made to the coast of North America in 1534. On this journey, Cartier came to Prince Edward Island, where* Anne of Green Gables *is set.*

Before you read, you should know that guillemots are birds related to the now-extinct great auk, which looked a little bit like a penguin. Gannets are seabirds that look something like seagulls, and eider ducks are sea ducks that live in cold areas. "Eiderdown," a kind of duck feather used to stuff mattresses, is named after the eider duck.

As he sailed northwards, past the deeply indented fiords and bays of eastern Newfoundland (the shores of which were still hugged by the winter ice), he and his men were much impressed with the incredible numbers of the sea fowl settled for nesting purposes on the rocky islands, especially on Funk Island. These birds were guillemots, puffins, great auks, gannets (called by Cartier *margaulx*), and probably gulls and eider duck. To his sailors—always hungry and partly fed on salted provisions, as seamen were down to a few years ago—this inexhaustible supply of fresh food was a source of great enjoyment. They were indifferent, no doubt, to the fishy flavour of the auks and the guillemots, and only noticed that they were splendidly fat. Moreover, the birds attracted polar bears "as large as cows and as white as swans." The bears would swim off from the shore to the islands (unless they could reach them by crossing the ice), and the sailors occasionally killed the bears and ate their flesh, which they compared in excellence and taste to veal.

Passing through the Straits of Belle Isle, Cartier's ships entered the Gulf of St. Lawrence. They had previously visited the adjoining coast of Labrador, and there had encountered their first natives, members of some Algonquin tribe from Canada, who had come north for seal fishing (Cartier is clever enough to notice and describe their birch-bark canoes). After examining the west coast of Newfoundland, Cartier's ships sailed on past the Magdalen Islands (stopping every now and then off some islet to collect supplies of sea birds, for the rocky ground was covered with them as thickly as a meadow with grass). On the shores of these islands they noticed "several great beasts like oxen, which have two tusks in the mouth similar to those of the elephant." These were walruses.

He reached the north coast of Prince Edward Island, and this lovely country received from him an enthusiastic description. The pine trees, the junipers, yews, elms, poplars, ash, and willows, the beeches and the maples, made the forest not only full of delicious and stimulating odours, but lovely in its varied tints of green. In the natural meadows and forest clearings there were red and white currants, gooseberries, strawberries, raspberries, a vetch which produced edible peas, and a grass with a grain like rye. The forest abounded in pigeons, and the climate was pleasant and warm.

Date ____________________

Name ____________________

Original Sentence Exercise

From *Pioneers in Canada* by Harry Johnston

Date ______________________________

Name ____

Week 28
Day Four

Dictation Exercise

Date ____________________

Name ____________________

Week 28
Day Five

Creative Writing

This page is left blank intentionally.

From *Young Folks' History of England*

by Charlotte Yonge

This story about the Romans in Britain was written a hundred and fifty years ago.

Julius Caesar heard that a little way off there was a country nobody knew anything about, except that the people were very fierce and savage, and that a sort of pearl was found in the shells of mussels which lived in the rivers. He could not bear that there should be any place that his own people, the Romans, did not know and subdue. So he commanded the ships to be prepared, and he and his soldiers embarked, watching the white cliffs on the other side of the sea grow higher and higher as he came nearer and nearer.

When he came quite up to them, he found the savages were there in earnest. They were tall men, with long red streaming hair, and such clothes as they had were woollen, checked like plaid; but many had their arms and breasts naked, and painted all over in blue patterns. They yelled and brandished their darts, to make Julius Caesar and his Roman soldiers keep away; but he only went on to a place where the shore was not quite so steep, and there commanded his soldiers to land. The savages had run along the shore too, and there was a terrible fight; but at last the man who carried the eagle standard for Caesar jumped down into the middle of the natives, calling out to his fellows that they must come after him, or they would lose their eagle. They all came rushing and leaping down, and thus they managed to force back the savages, and make their way to the shore.

There was not much worth having when they had made their way there. Though they came again the next year, and forced their way a good deal farther into the country, they saw chiefly bare downs, or heaths, or thick woods. The few houses were little more than piles of stones, and the people were rough and wild, and could do very little. The men hunted wild boars, and wolves and stags, and the women dug the ground, and raised a little corn, which they ground to flour between two stones to make bread; and they spun the wool of their sheep, dyed it with bright colors, and wove it into dresses. They had some strong places in the woods, with trunks of trees, cut down to shut them in from the enemy, with all their flocks and cattle; but Caesar did not get into any of these. He only made the natives give him some of their pearls, and call the Romans their masters, and then he went back to his ships, and none of the set of savages who were alive when he came saw him or his Romans any more.

Do you know who these savages were who fought with Julius Caesar? They were called Britons. And the country he came to see? That was our very own island, England, only it was not called so then. And the place where Julius Caesar landed is called Deal, and, if you look at the map where England and France most nearly touch one another, I think you will see the name Deal, and remember it was there Julius Caesar landed, and fought with the Britons.

Date ____________________

Name ____

Narration Exercise

From *Young Folks' History of England* by Charlotte Yonge

Date ______________________

Week 29
Day Two

Name ____

Dictation Exercise

From *Young Folks' History of England*
by Charlotte Yonge

This selection continues the story of the Romans in Britain.

It was nearly a hundred years before any more of the Romans came to Britain; but they were people who could not hear of a place without wanting to conquer it, and they never left off trying till they had done what they undertook.

The Romans made beautiful straight roads all over the country, and they built towns. Almost all the towns whose names end in *-chester* were begun by the Romans, and bits of their walls are to be seen still, built of very small bricks. Sometimes people dig up a bit of the beautiful pavement of colored tiles, in patterns, which used to be the floors of their houses, or a piece of their money, or one of their ornaments.

For the Romans held Britain for four hundred years, and tamed the wild people in the south, and taught them to speak and dress, and read and write like themselves, so that they could hardly be known from the Romans. Only the wild ones beyond the wall, and in the mountains, were as savage as ever, and, now and then, used to come and steal the cattle, and burn the houses of their neighbors who had learnt better.

Another set of wild people used to come over in boats across the North Sea and German Ocean. These people had their home in the country that is called Holstein and Jutland. They were tall men, and had blue eyes and fair hair, and they were very strong, and good-natured in a rough sort of way, though they were fierce to their enemies. There was a great deal more fighting than any one has told us about; but the end of it all was that the Roman soldiers were wanted at home, and though the great British chief we call King Arthur fought very bravely, he could not drive back the blue-eyed men in the ships; but more and more came, till, at last, they got all the country, and drove the Britons, some up into the north, some into the mountains that rise along the west of the island, and some into its west point.

The Britons used to call the blue-eyed men Saxons; but they called themselves Angles, and the country was called after them Angle-land. Don't you know what it is called now? England itself, and the people English. They spoke much the same language as we do.

As to the Britons, the English went on driving them back till they only kept their mountains. There they have gone on living ever since, and talking their own old language. The English called them Welsh, a name that meant strangers, and we call them Welsh still, and their country Wales. They made a great many grand stories about their last brave chief, Arthur, till, at last, they turned into a sort of fairy tale. It was said that, when King Arthur lay badly wounded after his last battle, he bade his friend fling his sword into the river, and that then three lovely ladies came in a boat, and carried him away to a secret island. The Welsh kept on saying, for years and years, that one day King Arthur would wake up again, and give them back all Britain, which used to be their own before the English got it for themselves; but the English have had England now for thirteen hundred years.

Date ______________________

Name ____

Week 29
Day Three

Original Sentence Exercise

From *Young Folks' History of England* by Charlotte Yonge

Date

Name

Week 29
Day Four

Dictation Exercise

Date ____________________

Name ____

Creative Writing

This page is left blank intentionally.

From *The Black Stallion*

by Walter Farley

At the beginning of The Black Stallion, *young Alec Ramsay is sailing home on a steamship, the* Drake, *after visiting an uncle in India. He is fascinated by a horse which is also travelling on the* Drake; *the horse is a black stalllion, wild and hard to manage.*

The Drake *is in the middle of the ocean when a storm sweeps down on it, late one night, and the ship begins to sink.*

Immediately Alec thought of the Black. What was happening to him? Was he still in his stall? Alec fought his way out of line and toward the stern of the boat. If the stallion was alive, he was going to set him free and give him his chance to fight for life.

The stall was still standing. Alec heard a shrill whistle rise above the storm. He rushed to the door, lifted the heavy bar, and swung it open. For a second the mighty hoofs stopped pounding and there was silence. Alec backed slowly away.

Then he saw the Black, his head held high, his nostrils blown out with excitement. Suddenly he snorted and plunged straight for the rail and Alec. Alec was paralyzed. He couldn't move. One hand was on the rail, which was broken at this point, leaving nothing between him and the open water. The Black swerved as he came near him, and the boy realized that the stallion was making for the hole. The horse's shoulder grazed him as he swerved, and Alec went flying into space. He felt the water close over his head.

When he came up, his first thought was of the ship; then he heard an explosion, and he saw the *Drake* settling deep into the water. Frantically he looked around for a lifeboat, but there was none in sight. Then he saw the Black swimming not more than ten yeards away. Something swished by him—a rope, and it was attached to the Black's halter! The same rope that they had used to bring the stallion aboard the boat, and which they had never been able to get close enough to the horse to untie. Without stopping to think, Alec grabbed hold of it. Then he was pulled through the water, into the oncoming seas.

The waves were still large, but with the aid of his life jacket, Alec was able to stay on top. He was too tired now to give much thought to what he had done. He only knew that he had had his choice of remaining in the water alone or being pulled by the Black. If he was to die, he would rather die with the mighty stallion than alone. He took one last look behind and saw the *Drake* sink into the depths.

For hours Alec battled the waves. He had tied the rope securely around his waist. He could hardly hold his head up. Suddenly he felt the rope slacken. The

Black had stopped swimming! Alec anxiously waited; peering into the darkness he could just make out the head of the stallion. The Black's whistle pierced the air! After a few minutes, the rope became taut again. The horse had changed his direction. Another hour passed, then the storm diminished to high, rolling swells. The first streaks of dawn appeared on the horizon.

The Black had stopped four times during the night, and each time he had altered his course. Alec wondered whether the stallion's wild instinct was leading him to land. The sun rose and shone down brightly on the boy's head; the salt water he had swallowed during the night made him sick to his stomach. But when Alec felt that he could hold out no longer, he looked at the struggling, fighting animal in front of him, and new courage came to him.

Suddenly he realized that they were going with the waves, instead of against them. He shoook his head, trying to clear his mind. Yes, they were riding in; they must be approaching land!

Date ____________________

Name ____

Week 30
Day One

Narration Exercise

From *The Black Stallion* by Walter Farley

Date ______________________

Name ____

Week 30
Day Two

Dictation Exercise

From *The Black Stallion*

by Walter Farley

Alec and the Black are marooned together on the island. It takes Alec a long time to make friends with the Black—and even longer before he dares to try and ride the stallion. The first time he mounts the Black, the horse throws him off immediately.

Alec waited for a few minutes—then once again led the stallion to the sand dune. His hand grasped the horse's mane. But this time he laid only the upper part of his body on thc stallion's back, while he talked soothingly into his ear. The Black flirted his ears back and forth as he glanced backward with his dark eyes.

"See, I'm not going to hurt you," Alec murmured, knowing that it was he who might be hurt. After a few minutes, Alec cautiously slid onto his back. Once again, the stallion snorted and sent the boy flying through the air.

Alec picked himself up from the ground—slower this time. But when he had rested, he whistled for the Black again. The stallion moved toward him. Alec determinedly stepped on the sand dune and once again let the Black feel his weight. Gently he spoke into a large ear, "It's me. I'm not much to carry." He slid onto the stallion's back. One arm slipped around the Black's neck as he half-reared. Then, like a shot from a gun, the Black broke down the beach. His action shifted, and his huge strides seemed to make him fly through the air.

Alec clung to the stallion's mane for his life. The wind screamed by and he couldn't see! Suddenly the Black swerved and headed up the sand dune; he reached the top and then down. The spring was a blur as they whipped by. To the rocks he raced, and then the stallion made a wide circle—his speed never diminishing. Down through a long ravine he rushed. Alec's blurred vision made out a black object in front of them, and as a flash he remembered the deep gully that was there. He felt the stallion gather himself; instinctively he leaned forward and held the Black firm and steady with his hands and knees. Then they were in the air, sailing over the black hole. Alec almost lost his balance when they landed, but recovered himself in time to keep from falling off! Once again the stallion reached the beach, his hoofbeats regular and rhythmic on the white sand.

The jump had helped greatly in clearing Alec's mind. He leaned closer to the stallion's ear and kept repeating, "Easy, Black. Easy." The stallion seemed to glide over the sand and then his speed began to lessen. Alec kept talking to him. Slower and slower ran the Black. Gradually he came to a stop. The boy released his grip from the stallion's mane and his arms encircled the Black's neck. He was weak with exhaustion—in no condition for such a ride! Wearily he slipped to the ground. Never had he dreamed a horse could run so fast! The stallion looked at him, his head held high, his large body only slightly covered with sweat.

That night Alec lay wide awake, his body aching with pain, but his heart pounding with excitement. He had ridden the Black! He had conquered this wild, unbroken stallion with kindness. He felt sure that from that day on the Black was his—his alone! But for what—would they ever be rescued? Would he ever see his home again? Alec shook his head. He had promised himself he wouldn't think of that any more.

Date ______________________

Name ______________________

Original Sentence Exercise

From *The Black Stallion* by Walter Farley

Date ____________________

Name ____________________

Week 30
Day Four

Dictation Exercise

Date ____________________

Name ____

Week 30
Day Five

Creative Writing

This page is left blank intentionally.

From *King Arthur and His Knights of the Round Table*

by Roger Lancelyn Green

This is from Roger Lancelyn Green's retelling of the legends about Arthur. The king of Britain who came before Arthur, Uther Pendragon, has just died without naming an heir, and Britain has fallen into disorder.

Then the land fell upon days more evil and wretched than any which had gone before. King Uther's knights fought amongst themselves, quarrelling as to who should rule; and the Saxons, seeing that there was no strong man to lead the Britons against them, conquered more and more of Britain.

Years of strife and misery went by, until the appointed time was at hand. Then Merlin, the good enchanter, came out from the deep, mysterious valleys of North Wales, which in those days was called Gwynedd, through Powys or South Wales, and passed on his way to London. And so great was his fame that neither Saxon nor Briton dared molest him.

Merlin came to London and spoke with the Archbishop; and a great gathering of knights was called for Christmas Day—so great that all of them could not find a place in the abbey church, so that some were forced to gather in the churchyard.

In the middle of the service, there arose suddenly a murmur of wonder outside the abbey: for there was seen, though no man saw it come, a great square slab of marble-stone in the churchyard, and on the stone an anvil of iron, and set point downwards a great, shining sword of steel thrust deeply into the anvil.

"Stir not till the service be done," commanded the Archbishop when this marvel was made known to him. "But pray the more unto God that we may find a remedy for the sore wounds of our land."

When the service was ended, the Archbishop and the lords and knights who had been within the abbey came out to see the wonder of the sword. Round about the anvil they found letters of gold set in the great stone, and the letters read thus:

WHOSO PULLETH OUT THIS SWORD FROM THIS STONE AND ANVIL IS THE TRUE-BORN KING OF ALL BRITAIN.

When they saw this, many and many a man tried to pull out the sword—but not one of them could stir it a hair's breadth.

"He is not here," said the Archbishop. "But doubt not that God will send us our King. Let messengers be sent through all the land to tell what is written on the stone: and upon New Year's Day we will hold a great tournament, and see whether our King is amongst those who come to joust. Until then, I counsel that we appoint ten knights to guard the stone, and set a rich pavilion over it."

All this was done, and upon New Year's Day a great host of knights met together. But none as yet could draw forth the sword out of the stone. Then they went all a little way off, and pitched tents, and held a tournament or sham-fight, trying their strength and skill at jousting with long lances of wood, or fighting with broad-swords.

Date ____________________

Name ______________________________________

Week 31
Day One

Narration Exercise

From *King Arthur and His Knights of the Round Table* by Roger Lancelyn Green

Date ____________________

Name ____

Week 31
Day Two

Dictation Exercise

From *King Arthur and His Knights of the Round Table*

by Roger Lancelyn Green

The story of Arthur, continued.

It happened that among those who came was the good knight Sir Ector, and his son Kay, who had been made a knight not many months before; and with them came Arthur, Sir Kay's young brother, a youth of scarcely sixteen years of age.

Riding to the jousts, Sir Kay found suddenly that he had left his sword in his lodgings, and he asked Arthur to ride back and fetch it for him.

"Certainly I will," said Arthur, who was always ready to do anything for other people, and back he rode to the town. But Sir Kay's mother had locked the door, and gone out to see the tournament, so that Arthur could not get into the lodgings at all.

This troubled Arthur very much. "My brother Kay must have a sword," he thought, as he rode slowly back. "It will be a shame and a matter for unkind jests if so young a knight comes to the jousts without a sword. But where can I find him one?...I know! I saw one sticking in an anvil in the churchyard, I'll fetch that: it's doing no good there!"

So Arthur set spurs to his horse and came to the churchyard. Tying his horse to the stile, he ran to the tent which had been set over the stone—and found that all ten of the guardian knights had also gone to the tournament. Without stopping to read what was written on the stone, Arthur pulled out the sword at a touch, ran back to his horse, and in a few minutes had caught up with Sir Kay and handed it over to him.

Arthur knew nothing of what sword it was, but Kay had already tried to pull it from the anvil, and saw at a glance that it was the same one. Instantly he rode to his father Sir Ector and said:

"Sir! Look, here is the sword out of the stone! So you see I must be the true-born King of all Britain!"

But Sir Ector knew better than to believe Sir Kay too readily. Instead, he rode back with him to the church, and there made him swear a solemn oath with his hands on the Bible to say truly how he came by the sword.

"My brother Arthur brought it to me," said Kay, with a sigh.

"And how did *you* get the sword?" asked Sir Ector.

"Sir, I will tell you," said Arthur, fearing that he had done wrong. "Kay sent me to fetch his sword, but I could not come to it. Then I remembered having seen this sword sticking uselessly into an anvil in the churchyard. I thought it could be put to a better use in my brother's hand—so I fetched it."

"Did you find no knights guarding the sword?" asked Sir Ector.

"Never a one," said Arthur.

"Well, put the sword back into the anvil, and let us see you draw it out," commanded Sir Ector.

"That's easily done," said Arthur, puzzled by all this trouble over a sword, and he set it back easily into the anvil.

Then Sir Kay seized it by the hilt and pulled his hardest: but struggle and strain as he might, he could not move it by a hair's breadth. Sir Ector tried also, but with no better success.

"Pull it out," he said to Arthur.

And Arthur, more and more bewildered, put his hand to the hilt and drew forth the sword as if out of a well-greased scabbard.

"Now," said Sir Ector, kneeling before Arthur and bowing his head in reverence, "I understand that you and none other are the true-born King of this land."

Date ______________________

Name ____

Original Sentence Exercise

From *King Arthur and His Knights of the Round Table* by Roger Lancelyn Green

Date ____________________

Week 31
Day Four

Name ____

Dictation Exercise

Date ______________________

Name ____

Week 31
Day Five

Creative Writing

This page is left blank intentionally.

“The Valiant Little Tailor”

by Jacob and Wilhelm Grimm

This story is found in the collection made by the brothers Jacob and Wilhelm Grimm.

One summer’s morning a little tailor was sitting on his table by the window; he was in good spirits, and sewed with all his might. Then came a peasant woman down the street crying: “Good jams, cheap! Good jams, cheap!”

This rang pleasantly in the tailor’s ears; he stretched his delicate head out of the window, and called: “Come up here, dear woman; here you will get rid of your goods.” The woman came up the three steps to the tailor with her heavy basket, and he made her unpack all the pots for him. He inspected each one, lifted it up, put his nose to it, and at length said: “The jam seems to me to be good, so weigh me out four ounces, dear woman.”

The woman who had hoped to find a good sale, gave him what he desired, but went away quite angry and grumbling. “Now, this jam shall be blessed by God,” cried the little tailor, “and give me health and strength.” So he brought the bread out of the cupboard, cut himself a piece right across the loaf and spread the jam over it.

Then he said, “I will just finish the jacket before I take a bite.” He laid the bread near him, sewed on, and in his joy, made bigger and bigger stitches. In the meantime the smell of the sweet jam rose to where the flies were sitting in great numbers, and they were attracted and descended on it in hosts. “Hi! who invited you?” said the little tailor, and drove the unbidden guests away. The flies, however, would not be turned away, but came back again in ever-increasing companies.

The little tailor at last lost all patience, and drew a piece of cloth from the hole under his work-table, and saying: “Wait, and I will give it to you,” struck it mercilessly on them. When he drew it away and counted, there lay before him no fewer than seven, dead and with legs stretched out.

He could not help admiring his own bravery. “The whole town shall know of this!” he said. And the little tailor hastened to cut himself a belt, stitched it, and embroidered on it in large letters: ‘Seven at one stroke!’ “What, the town!” he continued, “the whole world shall hear of it!” and his heart wagged with joy like a lamb’s tail.

The tailor put on the belt, and resolved to go forth into the world, because he thought his workshop was too small for his valour. Before he went away, he sought about in the house to see if there was anything which he could take with him; however, he found nothing but an old cheese, and that he put in his pocket. In front of the door he observed a bird which had caught itself in the thicket. It had to go into his pocket with the cheese. Now he took to the road boldly, and as he was light and nimble, he felt no fatigue.

Date ______________________

Name ____

Narration Exercise

From "The Valiant Little Tailor" by the Brothers Grimm

Date

Name

Week 32
Day Two

Dictation Exercise

"The Valiant Little Tailor"

by Jacob and Wilhelm Grimm

This is the continuation of the story of the little tailor.

The road led him up a mountain, and when he had reached the highest point of it, there sat a powerful giant looking peacefully about him. The little tailor went bravely up, spoke to him, and said: "Good day, comrade, so you are sitting there overlooking the wide-spread world! I am just on my way thither, and want to try my luck. Have you any inclination to go with me?"

The giant looked contemptuously at the tailor, and said: "You ragamuffin! You miserable creature!"

"Oh, indeed?" answered the little tailor, and unbuttoned his coat, and showed the giant the belt, "There may you read what kind of a man I am!" The giant read: "Seven at one stroke," and thought that they had been men whom the tailor had killed, and began to feel a little respect for the tiny fellow.

The giant took a stone in his hand and squeezed it together so that water dropped out of it. "Do that likewise," said the giant, "if you have strength."

"Is that all?" said the tailor, "That is child's play with us!" and put his hand into his pocket, brought out the soft cheese, and pressed it until the liquid ran out of it. "Faith," said he, "that was a little better, wasn't it?"

The giant did not know what to say, and could not believe it of the little man. Then the giant picked up a stone and threw it so high that the eye could scarcely follow it. "Now, little mite of a man, do that likewise," he said.

"Well thrown," said the tailor, "but after all the stone came down to earth again; I will throw you one which shall never come back at all," and he put his hand into his pocket, took out the bird, and threw it into the air. The bird, delighted with its liberty, rose, flew away and did not come back. "How does that shot please you, comrade?" asked the tailor.

"You can certainly throw," said the giant, "but now we will see if you are able to carry anything properly." He took the little tailor to a mighty oak tree which lay there felled on the ground, and said: "If you are strong enough, help me to carry the tree out of the forest."

"Readily," answered the little man. "Take you the trunk on your shoulders, and I will raise up the branches and twigs; after all, they are the heaviest." The giant took the trunk on his shoulder, but the tailor seated himself on a branch, and the giant, who could not look round, had to carry away the whole tree, and the little tailor into the bargain: he behind, was quite merry and happy, and whistled the song: "Three tailors rode forth from the gate," as if carrying the tree were child's play.

The giant, after he had dragged the heavy burden part of the way, could go no further, and cried: "Hark you, I shall have to let the tree fall!"

The tailor sprang nimbly down, seized the tree with both arms as if he had been carrying it, and said to the giant: "You are such a great fellow, and yet cannot even carry the tree!"

Date ____________________

Name ______________________________________

Week 32
Day Three

Original Sentence Exercise

From "The Valiant Little Tailor" by the Brothers Grimm

Date ______________________________

Name ____

Dictation Exercise

Date ____________________

Name ______________________________________

Week 32
Day Five

Creative Writing

This page is left blank intentionally.

From *Bambi: A Life in the Woods*

by Felix Salten

You may have seen the cartoon movie Bambi. *That movie was made from a wonderful book, written by Felix Salten. The book is much more interesting than the movie! It is called* Bambi: A Life in the Woods. *In this first selection, the newborn young deer is coming to the meadow with his mother for the first time.*

Presently he began to enjoy the meadow with his eyes also. Its wonders amazed him at every step he took. You could not see the tiniest speck of earth the way you could in the forest. Blade after blade of grass covered every inch of the ground. It tossed and waved luxuriantly. It bent softly aside under every footstep, only to rise up unharmed again. The broad green meadow was starred with white daisies, with the thick, round red and purple clover blossoms and bright golden dandelion heads.

"Look, look, Mother!" Bambi exclaimed. "There's a flower flying."

"That's not a flower," said his mother, "that's a butterfly."

Bambi stared at the butterfly entranced. It had darted lightly from a blade of grass and was fluttering about in its giddy way. Then Bambi saw that there were many butterflies flying in the air above the meadow. They seemed to be in a hurry and yet moved slowly, fluttering up and down in a sort of game that delighted him. They really did look like gay flying flowers that would not stay on their stems but had unfastened themselves in order to dance a little. They looked, too, like flowers that come to rest at sundown but have no fixed places and have to hunt for them, dropping down and vanishing as if they really had settled somewhere, yet always flying up again, a little way at first, then higher and higher, and always searching farther and farther because all the good places have already been taken.

Bambi gazed at them all. He would have loved to see one close by. He wanted to see one face to face but he could not. They flew in and out continually. The air was aflutter with them.

When he looked down at the ground again he was delighted with the thousands of living things he saw stirring under his hoofs. They ran and jumped in all directions. He would see a wild swarm of them, and the next moment they had disappeared in the grass again.

"Who are they, Mother?" he asked.

"Those are ants," his mother answered.

"Look," cried Bambi, "see that piece of grass jumping. Look how high it can jump!"

"That's not grass," his mother explained, "that's a nice grasshopper."

"Why does he jump that way?" asked Bambi.

"Because we're walking here," his mother answered; "he's afraid we'll step on him."

"Oh," said Bambi, turning to the grasshopper, who was sitting on a daisy; "oh," he said again politely, "you don't have to be afraid; we won't hurt you."

"I'm not afraid," the grasshopper replied in a quavering voice; "I was only frightened for a moment when I was talking to my wife."

"Excuse us for disturbing you," said Bambi shyly.

"Not at all," the grasshopper quavered. "Since it's you, its perfectly all right. But you never know who's coming and you have to be careful."

"This is the first time in my life that I've ever been on the meadow," Bambi explained; "my mother brought me..."

The grasshopper was sitting with his head lowered as though he were going to butt. He put on a serious face and murmured, "That doesn't interest me at all. I haven't time to stand here gossiping with you. I have to be looking for my wife. Hopp!" And he gave a jump.

"Hopp!" said Bambi in surprise at the high jump with which the grasshopper vanished.

Date ____________________

Name ______________________________________

Narration Exercise

From *Bambi: A Life in the Woods* by Felix Salten

Date ____________________

Name ____

Week 33
Day Two

Dictation Exercise

From *Bambi: A Life in the Woods*

by Felix Salten

One evening Bambi was roaming about the meadow again with his mother. He thought that he knew everything there was to see or hear there. But in reality it appeared that he did not know as much as he thought.

This time was just like the first. Bambi played tag with his mother. He ran around in circles, and the open space, the deep sky, the fresh air intoxicated him so that he grew perfectly wild. After a while he noticed that his mother was standing still. He stopped short in the middle of a leap so suddenly that his four legs spread far apart. To get his balance he bounded high into the air and then stood erect. His mother seemed to be talking to someone he couldn't make out through the tall grass. Bambi toddled up inquisitively.

Two long ears were moving in the tangled grass stems close to his mother. They were grayish brown and prettily marked with black stripes. Bambi stopped, but his mother said, "Come here. This is our friend, the Hare. Come here like a nice boy and let him see you."

Bambi went over. There sat the Hare looking like a very honest creature. At times his long spoonlike ears stood bolt upright. At others they fell back limply as though they had suddenly grown weak. Bambi became somewhat critical as he looked at the whiskers that stood out so stiff and straight on both sides of the Hare's mouth. But he noticed that the Hare had a very mild face and extremely good-natured features and that he cast timid glances at the world from out of his big round eyes. The Hare really did look friendly. Bambi's passing doubts vanished immediately. But oddly enough, he had lost all the respect he originally felt for the Hare.

"Good evening, young man," the Hare greeted him, with studied politeness.

Bambi merely nodded good evening. He didn't understand why, but he simply nodded. He was very friendly and civil, but a little condescending. He could not help himself. Perhaps he was born that way.

"What a charming young prince," said the Hare to Bambi's mother. He looked at Bambi attentively, raising first one spoonlike ear, then the other, and then both of them, and letting them fall again, suddenly and limply, which didn't please Bambi. The motion of the Hare's ears seemed to say, "He isn't worth bothering with."

Meanwhile the Hare continued to study Bambi with his big round eyes. His nose and his mouth with the handsome whiskers moved incessantly in the same way a man who is trying not to sneeze twitches his nose and lips. Bambi had to laugh.

The Hare laughed quickly, too, but his eyes grew more thoughtful. "I congratulate you," he said to Bambi's mother. "I sincerely congratulate you on your son. Yes, indeed, he'll make a splendid prince in time. Anyone can see that."

To Bambi's boundless surprise he suddenly sat straight on his hind legs. After he had spied all around with his ears stiffened and his nose constantly twitching, he sat down decently on all fours again. "Now if you good people will excuse me," he said at last, "I have all kinds of things to do tonight. If you'll be so good as to excuse me...." He turned away and hopped off with his ears back so that they touched his shoulders.

Date ______________________

Name ____

Week 33
Day Three

Original Sentence Exercise

From *Bambi: A Life in the Woods* by Felix Salten

Date ____________________

Name ____________________

Week 33
Day Four

Dictation Exercise

Date ______________________

Name ____

Week 33
Day Five

Creative Writing

This page is left blank intentionally.

"Prince Wicked and the Grateful Animals" from *More Jataka Tales*

by Ellen Babbitt

The Jataka Tales are traditional stories from India. This story was retold about a hundred years ago by Ellen Babbitt. You'll read the first half of the story today, and the rest of it later in the week.

Once upon a time a king had a son named Prince Wicked. He was fierce and cruel, and he spoke to nobody without abuse, or blows. Like grit in the eye, was Prince Wicked to every one, both in the palace and out of it.

His people said to one another, "If he acts this way while he is a prince, how will he act when he is king?"

One day when the prince was swimming in the river, suddenly a great storm came on, and it grew very dark.

In the darkness the servants who were with the prince swam from him, saying to themselves, "Let us leave him alone in the river, and he may drown."

When they reached the shore, some of the servants who had not gone into the river said, "Where is Prince Wicked?"

"Isn't he here?" they asked. "Perhaps he came out of the river in the darkness and went home." Then the servants all went back to the palace.

The king asked where his son was, and again the servants said: "Isn't he here, O King? A great storm came on soon after we went into the water. It grew very dark. When we came out of the water the prince was not with us."

At once the king had the gates thrown open. He and all his men searched up and down the banks of the river for the missing prince. But no trace of him could be found.

In the darkness the prince had been swept down the river. He was crying for fear he would drown when he came across a log. He climbed upon the log, and floated farther down the river.

When the great storm arose, the water rushed into the homes of a Rat and a Snake who lived on the river bank. The Rat and the Snake swam out into the river and found the same log the prince had found. The Snake climbed upon one end of the log, and the Rat climbed upon the other.

On the river's bank a cottonwood-tree grew, and a young Parrot lived in its branches. The storm pulled up this tree, and it fell into the river. The heavy rain beat down the Parrot when it tried to fly, and it could not go far. Looking down it saw the log and flew down to rest. Now there were four on the log floating down stream together.

Just around the bend in the river a certain poor man had built himself a hut. As he walked to and fro late at night listening to the storm, he heard the loud cries of the prince. The poor man said to himself: "I must get that man out of the water. I must save his life." So he shouted: "I will save you! I will save you!" as he swam out in the river.

Soon he reached the log, and pushing it by one end, he soon pushed it into the bank. The prince jumped up and down, he was so glad to be safe and sound on dry land.

Then the poor man saw the Snake, the Rat, and the Parrot, and carried them to his hut. He built a fire, putting the animals near it so they could get dry. He took care of them first, because they were the weaker, and afterwards he looked after the comfort of the prince.

Then the poor man brought food and set it before them, looking after the animals first and the prince afterwards. This made the young prince angry, and he said to himself: "This poor man does not treat me like a prince. He takes care of the animals before taking care of me." Then the prince began to hate the poor man.

A few days later, when the prince, and the Snake, the Rat, and the Parrot were rested, and the storm was all over, the Snake said good-by to the poor man with these words:

"Father, you have been very kind to me. I know where there is some buried gold. If ever you want gold, you have only to come to my home and call, 'Snake!' and I will show you the buried gold. It shall all be yours."

Next the Rat said good-by to the poor man. "If ever you want money," said the Rat, "come to my home, and call out, 'Rat!' and I will show you where a great deal of money is buried near my home. It shall all be yours."

Then the Parrot came, saying: "Father, silver and gold have I none, but if you ever want choice rice, come to where I live and call, 'Parrot!' and I will call all my family and friends together, and we will gather the choicest rice in the fields for you."

Last came the prince. In his heart he hated the poor man who had saved his life. But he pretended to be as thankful as the animals had been, saying, "Come to me when I am king, and I will give you great riches." So saying, he went away.

Date ______________________

Name ______________________

Week 34
Day One

Narration Exercise

From "Prince Wicked and the Grateful Animals" by Ellen Babbitt

Date

Week 34
Day Two

Name

Dictation Exercise

"Prince Wicked and the Grateful Animals"
from *More Jataka Tales*
by Ellen Babbitt

Today we'll finish the story of Prince Wicked.

Not long after this the prince's father died, and Prince Wicked was made king. He was then very rich.

By and by the poor man said to himself: "Each of the four whose lives I saved made a promise to me. I will see if they will keep their promises."

First of all he went to the Snake, and standing near his hole, the poor man called out, "Snake!"

At once the Snake darted forth, and with every mark of respect he said: "Father, in this place there is much gold. Dig it up and take it all."

"Very well," said the poor man. "When I need it, I will not forget."

After visiting for a while, the poor man said good-by to the Snake, and went to where the Rat lived, calling out, "Rat!"

The Rat came at once, and did as the Snake had done, showing the poor man where the money was buried.

"When I need it, I will come for it," said the poor man.

Going next to the Parrot, he called out, "Parrot!" and the bird flew down from the tree-top as soon as he heard the call.

"O Father," said the Parrot, "shall I call together all my family and friends to gather choice rice for you?"

The poor man, seeing that the Parrot was willing and ready to keep his promise, said: "I do not need rice now. If ever I do, I will not forget your offer."

Last of all, the poor man went into the city where the king lived. The king, seated on his great white elephant, was riding through the city. The king saw the poor man, and said to himself: "That poor man has come to ask me for the great riches I promised to give him. I must have his head cut off before he can tell the people how he saved my life when I was the prince."

So the king called his servants to him and said: "You see that poor man over there? Seize him and bind him, beat him at every corner of the street as you march him out of the city, and then chop off his head."

The servants had to obey their king. So they seized and bound the poor man. They beat him at every corner of the street. The poor man did not cry out, but he said, over and over again, "It is better to save poor, weak animals than to save a prince."

At last some wise men among the crowds along the street asked the poor man what prince he had saved. Then the poor man told the whole story, ending with the words, "By saving your king, I brought all this pain upon myself."

The wise men and all the rest of the crowd cried out: "This poor man saved the life of our king, and now the king has ordered him to be killed. How can we be sure that he will not have any, or all, of us killed? Let us kill him." And in their anger they rushed from every side upon the king as he rode on his elephant, and with arrows and stones they killed him then and there.

Then they made the poor man king, and set him to rule over them.

Name

Date

Week 34
Day Three

Original Sentence Exercise

From "Prince Wicked and the Grateful Animals" by Ellen Babbitt

Date ______________________

Name ____

Week 34
Day Four

Dictation Exercise

Date ______________________________

Name ____

Creative Writing

This page is left blank intentionally.

From *The Jungle Book*

by Rudyard Kipling

This story from The Jungle Book *tells about Mowgli, a young boy being raised by a wolf family in the jungle. His tutors are Bagheera the panther and Baloo the brown bear. Baloo has told Mowgli not to play with the monkeys, who are known to the jungle folk as "the Bandar-log." But Mowgli has ignored the bear and has run off to play with the monkeys—who kidnap him and haul him away!*

They belonged to the tree-tops, and as beasts very seldom look up, there was no occasion for the monkeys and the Jungle People to cross one another's path. But whenever they found a sick wolf, or a wounded tiger or bear, the monkeys would torment him, and would throw sticks and nuts at any beast for fun and in the hope of being noticed. Then they would howl and shriek senseless songs, and invite the Jungle People to climb up their trees and fight them, or would start furious battles over nothing among themselves, and leave the dead monkeys where the Jungle People could see them.

They were always just going to have a leader and laws and customs of their own, but they never did, because their memories would not hold over from day to day, and so they settled things by making up a saying: "What the Bandar-log think now the Jungle will think later": and that comforted them a great deal. None of the beasts could reach them, but on the other hand none of the beasts would notice them, and that was why they were so pleased when Mowgli came to play with them, and when they heard how angry Baloo was.

They never meant to do any more—the Bandar-log never mean anything at all—but one of them invented what seemed to him a brilliant idea, and he told all the others that Mowgli would be a useful person to keep in the tribe, because he could weave sticks together for protection from the wind; so, if they caught him, they could make him teach them. Of course Mowgli, as a wood-cutter's child, inherited all sorts of instincts, and used to make little play-huts of fallen branches without thinking how he came to do it. The Monkey People, watching in the trees, considered these huts most wonderful. This time, they said, they were really going to have a leader and become the wisest people in the jungle—so wise that every one else would notice and envy them. Therefore they followed Baloo and Bagheera and Mowgli through the jungle very quietly till it was time for the midday nap, and Mowgli, who was very much ashamed of himself, slept between the panther and the bear, resolving to have no more to do with the Monkey People.

The next thing he remembered was feeling hands on his legs and arms—hard, strong little hands—and then a swash of branches in his face; and then he was staring down through the swaying boughs as Baloo woke the jungle with his deep cries and Bagheera bounded up the trunk with every tooth bared. The Bandar-log howled with triumph, and scuffled away to the upper branches where Bagheera dared not follow, shouting: "He has noticed us! Bagheera has noticed us! All the Jungle People admire us for our skill and our cunning!" Then they began their flight; and the flight of the Monkey People through treeland is one of the things nobody can describe. They have their regular roads and cross-roads, uphills and downhills, all laid out from fifty to seventy or a hundred feet aboveground, and by these they can travel even at night if necessary.

Two of the strongest monkeys caught Mowgli under the arms and swung off with him through the tree-tops, twenty feet at a bound. Had they been alone they could have gone twice as fast, but the boy's weight held them back. Sick and giddy as Mowgli was he could not help enjoying the wild rush, though the glimpses of earth far down below frightened him, and the terrible check and jerk at the end of the swing over nothing but empty air brought his heart between his teeth.

His escort would rush him up a tree till he felt the weak topmost branches crackle and bend under them, and, then, with a cough and a whoop, would fling themselves into the air outward and downward, and bring up hanging by their hands or their feet to the lower limbs of the next tree. Sometimes he could see for miles and miles over the still green jungle, as a man on the top of a mast can see for miles across the sea, and then the branches and leaves would lash him across the face, and he and his two guards would be almost down to earth again.

So bounding and crashing and whooping and yelling, the whole tribe of Bandar-log swept along the tree-roads with Mowgli their prisoner.

Date ______________________

Name ______________________________________

Week 35
Day One

Narration Exercise

From *The Jungle Book* by Rudyard Kipling

Date ____________________

Name ____

Dictation Exercise

From *The Jungle Book*

by Rudyard Kipling

The monkeys have taken Mowgli to their headquarters, the Cold Lairs.

In the Cold Lairs the Monkey People were not thinking of Mowgli's friends at all. They had brought the boy to the Lost City, and were very pleased with themselves for the time. Mowgli had never seen an Indian city before, and though this was almost a heap of ruins it seemed very wonderful and splendid. Some king had built it long ago on a little hill. You could still trace the stone causeways that led up to the ruined gates where the last splinters of wood hung to the worn, rusted hinges. Trees had grown into and out of the walls; the battlements were tumbled down and decayed, and wild creepers hung out of the windows of the towers on the walls in bushy hanging clumps.

A great roofless palace crowned the hill, and the marble of the courtyards and the fountains was split and stained with red and green, and the very cobblestones in the courtyard where the king's elephants used to live had been thrust up and apart by grasses and young trees. From the palace you could see the rows and rows of roofless houses that made up the city, looking like empty honeycombs filled with blackness; the shapeless block of stone that had been an idol in the square where four roads met; the pits and dimples at street corners where the public wells once stood, and the shattered domes of temples with wild figs sprouting on their sides.

The monkeys called the place their city, and pretended to despise the Jungle People because they lived in the forest. And yet they never knew what the buildings were made for nor how to use them. They would sit in circles on the hall of the king's council-chamber, and scratch for fleas and pretend to be men; or they would run in and out of the roofless houses and collect pieces of plaster and old bricks in a corner, and forget where they had hidden them, and fight and cry in scuffling crowds, and then break off to play up and down the terraces of the king's garden, where they would shake the rose-trees and the oranges in sport to see the fruit and flowers fall. They explored all the passages and dark tunnels in the palace and the hundreds of little dark rooms; but they never remembered what they had seen and what they had not, and so drifted about in ones and twos or crowds, telling one another that they were doing as men did. They drank at the tanks and made the water all muddy, and then they fought over it, and then they would all rush together in mobs and shout: "There are none in the jungle so wise and good and clever and strong and gentle as the Bandar-log." Then all would begin again till they grew tired of the city and went back to the tree-tops, hoping the Jungle People would notice them.

Mowgli, who had been trained under the Law of the Jungle, did not like or understand this kind of life. The monkeys dragged him into the Cold Lairs late in the afternoon, and instead of going to sleep, as Mowgli would have done after a long journey, they joined hands and danced about and sang their foolish songs.

Date ____________________

Name ____________________

Original Sentence Exercise

From *The Jungle Book* by Rudyard Kipling

Date ____________________

Name ____________________

Week 35
Day Four

Dictation Exercise

Date ______________________

Name ______________________

Week 35
Day Five

Creative Writing

This page is left blank intentionally.

From *Rabbit Hill*

by Robert Lawson

This book was first published in 1944. It is the story of the animals who live on a deserted farm called the Hill. One of these animals is Little Georgie, a young rabbit who lives with his family beneath the Hill. In this excerpt, Little Georgie is hopping past a neighbor's house, not really paying attention, when the neighbor's dog, the Old Hound, surprises him and begins to chase him.

You should know that "Porkey" is the name of Georgie's friend the woodchuck, an animal also called a "groundhog" in some parts of the country.

Instinctively Little Georgie made several wide springs that carried him temporarily out of harm's way. He paused a fraction of a second to tighten the knapsack strap and then set off at a good steady pace. "Don't waste speed on a plodder" was Father's rule. He tried a few checks and doubles and circlings, although he knew they were pretty useless. The great fields were too bare, and the Old Hound knew all the tricks. No matter how he turned and dodged, the Old Hound was always there, coming along at his heavy gallop. He looked for Woodchuck burrows, but there were none in sight. "Well, I guess I'll have to run it out," said Little Georgie.

He pulled the knapsack strap tighter, laced back his ears, put his stomach to the ground, and RAN. And *how* he ran!

The warm sun had loosened his muscles; the air was invigorating; Little Georgie's leaps grew longer and longer. Never had he felt so young and strong. His legs were like coiled springs of steel that released themselves of their own accord. He was hardly conscious of any effort, only of his hind feet pounding the ground, and each time they hit, those wonderful springs released and shot him through the air. He sailed over fences and stone walls as though they were mole runs. Why, this was almost like flying! Now he understood what Zip the Swallow had been driving at when he tried to describe what it was like. He glanced back at the Old Hound, far behind now, but still coming along at his plodding gallop. He was old and must be tiring, while he, Little Georgie, felt stronger and more vigorous at every leap. Why didn't the old fool give up and go home?

And then, as he shot over the brow of a slight rise, he suddenly knew. *He had forgotten Deadman's Brook!* There it lay before him, broad and deep, curving out in a great silvery loop. He, the son of Father, gentleman hunter from the Bluegrass, had been driven into a trap, a trap that even Porkey should have been able to avoid! Whether he turned to right or left the loop of the creek hemmed him in and the Old Hound could easily cut him off. There was nothing for it but to jump!

This sickening realization had not reduced his speed; now he redoubled it. The slope helped, and his soaring leaps became prodigious. The wind whistled through his laced-back ears. Still he kept his head, as Father would have wished him to. He picked a spot where the bank was high and firm; he spaced his jumps so they would come out exactly right.

The take-off was perfect. He put every ounce of leg muscle into that final kick and sailed out into space. Below him he could see the cream-puff clouds mirrored in the dark water, he could see the pebbles on the bottom and the silver flash of frightened minnows dashing away from his flying shadow. Then, with a breath-taking thump, he landed, turned seven somersaults, and came up sitting in a clump of soft lush grass.

He froze, motionless except for heaving sides, and watched the Old Hound come thundering down the slope, slide to a stop and, after eyeing the water disgustedly, take his way slowly homeward, his dripping tongue almost dragging the ground.

Date ____________________

Name ____________________

Original Sentence Evaluation

From *Rabbit Hill* by Robert Lawson

Date ______________________

Name ____

Dictation Evaluation

PERMISSIONS

Caxton Press: Excerpts from *Paul Bunyan Swings His Axe*, by Dell McCormick. Copyright 1936, The Caxton Printers. Used by permission of Caxton Press, Caldwell, Idaho.

Scott Corbett: excerpts from *The Lemonade Trick*, by Scott Corbett, copyright 1960. Used by permission of Curtis Brown, Ltd.

Tom Doherty Associates, LLC: Excerpts from *The Furious Flycycle* by Jan Wahl, copyright 1968. Reprinted with permission of Tor Books, an imprint of Tom Doherty Associates, LLC.

William B. Eerdmans Publishing Company: Excerpts from *C.S. Lewis: The Man Behind Narnia*, by Beatrice Gormley. Copyright 1998 Beatrice Gormley. Used by permission of William B. Eerdmans Publishing Company.

Hachette Book Group: Excerpts from *Mr. Revere and I*, by Robert Lawson, copyright 1953/1981 Robert Lawson. Used with permission of Hachette Book Group.

Harcourt, Inc.: excerpts from *The Moffats*, by Eleanor Estes, copyright 1941, 1969.

HarperCollins Publishers LLC: "Stegosaurus," from *Tyrannosaurus Was a Beast*, by Jack Prelutsky, copyright 1992, HarperCollins.

HarperCollins Publishers LLC: Excerpts from *Farmer Boy* by Laura Ingalls Wilder. Copyright 1933, 1961 the Little House Trust.

HarperCollins Publishers LLC: Excerpts from *Mrs. Piggle-Wiggle's Magic*, by Betty MacDonald. Copyright 1949, 1977.

Henry Holt and Company, LLC: Excerpts from *Time Cat: The Remarkable Journeys of Jason and Gareth*, by Lloyd Alexander, text copyright © 1963, 1991 by Lloyd Alexander. Reprinted with permission of Henry Holt and Company, LLC. All rights reserved.

Henry Holt and Company, LLC: Excerpts from *The Four-Story Mistake* written and illustrated by Elizabeth Enright. Copyright © 1942 by Elizabeth Enright Gillham. Copyright renewed © 1970 by Nicholas W. Gillham, Robert Gillham II, and Oliver Gillham. Reprinted by permission of Henry Holt and Company. All rights reserved.

The C.S. Lewis Company, Ltd: Excerpts from *The Lion, the Witch and the Wardrobe*, by C.S. Lewis, copyright © 1950 C.S. Lewis Pte. Ltd. Extract reprinted by permission of C.S. Lewis Company Ltd.

Penguin Group USA: Excerpts from *And Then What Happened, Paul Revere?*, by Jean Fritz, illustrated by Margot Tomes, copyright © 1973 by Jean Fritz. Used by permission of G. P. Putnam's Sons, an imprint of Penguin Publishing Group, a division of Penguin Random House LLC. All rights reserved.

Penguin Group USA: Excerpts from *Homer Price*, by Robert McCloskey, copyright 1943, renewed © 1971 by Robert McCloskey. Used by permission of Viking Children's Books, an imprint of Penguin Young Readers Group, a division of Penguin Random House LLC. All rights reserved.

Penguin Group UK: Excerpts from *King Arthur and His Knights of the Round Table*, by Roger Lancelyn Green, copyright 1953. Used by permission of Penguin Group UK.

Penguin Group USA: Excerpts from *Rabbit Hill*, by Robert Lawson, copyright 1944 by Robert Lawson; renewed © 1972 by John W. Boyd. Used by permission of Viking Children's Books, an imprint of Penguin Young Readers Group, a Division of Penguin Random House LLC. All rights reserved.

Random House, Inc: Excerpts from *The Black Stallion*, by Walter Farley, text copyright 1941 by Walter Farley. Copyright © renewed 1969 by Walter Farley. Used by permission of Random House Children's Books, a division of Penguin Random House LLC. All rights reserved.

Random House, Inc: Excerpts from *Babe: The Gallant Pig,* by Dick King-Smith, text copyright 1983 by Dick King-Smith. Used by permission of Crown Publishers, an imprint of Random House Children's Books, a division of Penguin Random House LLC. All rights reserved.